BINDING CHAOS

MASS COLLABORATION ON A GLOBAL SCALE

HEATHER MARSH

With grateful appreciation to my patrons and my invaluable epistemic community:

Adam Kendall

Douglas Lucas

Fabiana Cecin

Connie Beckerley

Join the Binding Chaos community!

www.mustread.press

The Binding Chaos Series

A look at the world

Binding Chaos

The Ontology Quartet

Self – The Creation of Me, Them and Us

Life - Abstracting Divinity

Will – Free Will and Seductive Coercion

Consciousness – Shaping Reality

The Sociology Quartet

Person - The Theft of Self

Power - Great Men, Commoners, Witches and Wretches

Nation – The Fourth Age of Nations

Governance - Autonomy Diversity Society

The Institutions Quartet

Economy – The Power Economy

Law – Law and Chaos

Knowledge – Political Science

Technology - Code Will Rule

www.mustread.press

Ebook: 978-1-989783-35-1
Paperback: 978-1-989783-11-5
Hardcover: 978-1-989783-12-2

Table of contents

Table of figures

Note to reader

Ten years ago, I collected a few of the articles I had written since 2010 into a short book which I published online with an open copyright. The purpose of these articles was to explain my viewpoint to people I had been working with around the world, exploring ideas around political representation, the economy and other aspects of governance and collaboration. At that time, I had no idea that the daily downloads of this book would increase every year and it would be widely read by a much broader audience over a decade after its publication.

While I am grateful that this text is increasingly considered relevant, it contains a few archaisms and has its own formatting quirks. For this edition, I have kept the text intact and changed only the formatting and illustrations to be in keeping with the rest of the books in what is now a series. Archaisms may still exist, but the book is a product of its time and it seems wrong to change it now. There is a new *Afterword* where I contextualize some of this work. I have also added the new glossary which contains terms from the entire series. *Binding Chaos* is now the precursor to a much more in depth analysis of government, society and the universe itself.

I hope this book and the rest of the *Binding Chaos* series continue to be useful to others on their journeys!

H.

Defining boundaries

Chapter 1

Threaten world is long overdue for a completely new system of governance. If there was ever a need for political representation or a paternalistic and opaque authority, it has been removed by technology. Every political system we have tried has proven incapable of protecting human rights and dignity. Every political system we have tried has devolved into oligarchy. To effect the change we require immediately, to give individuals control and responsibility, to bring regional systems under regional governance, allow global collaboration and protect the heritage of future generations, we need a new political model.

Corporations have the freedom to live in a world without borders or social responsibility, to own property no individual can claim and to control a one world government and legal system. This has had insupportable consequences for the world's resources and individual rights. People are locked within arbitrary national borders by ever increasing surveillance, military and xenophobic propaganda, crippling our ability to collaborate and frequently, our ability to survive. Our naturally migratory species are being caged like zoo animals, increasingly even as technology makes it more possible for us to interact. Immigration has become a privilege of the elite instead of a right of the desperate. The world's people are being divided, not into naturally forming communities, but into corporate controlled economic markets. Governance by nation states is now as arbitrary and illogical as city states were earlier found to be.

The accelerated pace and power of global communication strains and bursts the old systems of control. People can walk en masse across borders, shun the current financial system, establish our own trade, create transparency and provide emergency assistance to each other. This power to dismantle the structures we have relied on is terrifying to many because there is no clear path ahead, and few structures have yet formed to replace the ones that are crumbling. The growth of extreme nationalists and traditionalists worldwide, the buildup of militaries and intelligence monitoring are indicative of this fear of our unknown future. Old authoritarian systems can no longer bind the natural chaos of a free society, but we can show the power of chaotic order, the beauty and creativity of collaborative freedom, if we build the right structures now.

The transference of old ideas to our new capabilities has so far mostly served to prove the ridiculousness of the old ideas, not provide alternatives. The hilarity of the Bitcoin stock market is a funhouse mirror of the old stock market but does not provide a marked difference in approach. The instant celebrity and celebrity power of social media is a more transparent and gameable but no less ridiculous version of celebrity influence. We now have the opportunity to create real alternatives for both economy and influence, for communication, collaboration and all tools of society. If we are unaware of the potential before us, we will not achieve everything we are capable of at this moment. What we are building with our software and laws at this time is nothing less than a completely new social structure. It deserves all of our attention.

This text is in no way meant to be a definitive answer to any of the questions before us. This is just a documentation of what seems apparent at this moment, what ideas have not worked and why, and what ideas seem to be working in isolated instances and may be able to scale to help us on a much wider basis in the future. A lot of these ideas are not what we thought would work only a couple of years ago when we tried for consensus on all things, anonymity, meritocracy, all decisions by assembly, peer to peer trade and the hive mind. Those ideals are all still wonderful and useful but require modifying to reflect what we have discovered in practice. Hopefully, we will evolve rapidly enough that the ideas here will also require modification immediately.

This text is also not a suggestion to usurp regional control or assembly and consensus process among local governments. It is looking for methods of mass collaboration which would allow us to effectively communicate and create on a global scale while still allowing us autonomy and regional choice.

Many ideas in this text are far more easily understood by the free software and hacker community than the world offline. The internet created an environment where it was possible to collaborate in ways that had never been tried before, to experiment with global participation, anonymity, a money free society, idea driven projects and many other methods that are still impossible or difficult in physical life. While the internet has many current structural problems that are hindering collaboration, the internet community

Humans are not machines, but their capabilities and inclinations will be guided by the limitations of the systems they are given to collaborate with.

is yet a generation ahead in experimenting with many of these concepts.

Humans are not machines, but their capabilities and inclinations will be guided by the limitations of the systems they are given to collaborate with. The structure of the code and the laws we write and the tools we create will decide the structure of our future societies as surely as landforms and villages decided societies in the past. The search for methodology in this book is more systems analysis than philosophy. We need structure we can actually code or build and the limitations of the internet, as our primary location of mass communication and collaboration, must be considered. It is not possible to have a pure data driven hierarchy in an ocean of data. There must be a method for us to filter out and fact check the most accepted ideas. All voices cannot be heard equally in an environment polluted by spam, astroturfing and sock puppets as they would in a local assembly, but they must all be heard. Decisions on how and what voices we amplify must be made carefully.

We need to recognize immediately the effect our future online tools will have on our future governance. Corporate ownership of our communication tools will cause us to yet again relinquish control to a landlord. Corporate sponsored voice amplification will lead to corporate controlled oligarchy. The ties of server based systems and registered domains make censorship possible and hierarchy unavoidable. The limitations to speech we allow to be imposed on us now will impact our governance as surely as moats and mountains did in the past.

Heather Marsh

The problem with democracy

Chapter 2

A round the world, people lamenting the demise of democracy, or fighting for the birth of 'true' democracy need to take a closer look. Democracy is a universally failed concept, not because we have not implemented it properly but because the ideas were flawed to begin with. Advocates of democracy as a system of governance usually hold that it will produce the greatest satisfaction among the governed by allowing the voices of all to be heard. If democracy was implemented in the way it is intended by any common definition to be implemented, the resulting society would not allow all voices to be heard and it could not be considered either fair or enlightened.

'True' democracy is at best only one step removed from ochlocracy or mob rule. In a society where the majority create the laws, the laws can always be changed to allow for the Salem witch trials, the current Guantanamo military commissions, or many other examples where mass panic allowed the revocation of years of law in order to persecute a minority. The celebration of democracy in Burma did not prevent the genocide of the Rohingya people[1], democracy in the United States does nothing to protect non-US citizens being attacked by the US military, and democracy in Egypt leaves almost half the population living under a social contract they are vehemently opposed to. There are two options commonly held to be our democratic choices: direct or representative democracy.

Chapter 3

Direct Democracy

A pure direct democracy is a pure tyranny of the majority. When a majority rules, there is no need for compromise and a minority will have their needs unrepresented, resulting in governance by the majority, not governance by the people. As in all systems where groups hold the highest power, individual rights are always at risk.

A direct democracy is impossible in actuality as no one can have the time to participate in every decision concerning them, and certainly not to educate themselves to provide meaningful input in every decision. To make the best decisions, expertise is required on each topic. Direct democracy does not always provide the best solutions. It provides the most popular, the most expedient, or even the most advertised solutions, more frequently as the decision becomes more complex.

Direct democracy gives equal weight to all votes, the expert and the novice, the completely dependent and the unaffected. Expert opinion is overshadowed by volume, which negatively impacts the resulting decisions. Allowing votes by people unaffected by the issue at hand results in not just uninformed decisions but also persecution of minorities.

Direct democracy is very susceptible to a hidden oligarchy, as those at the bottom of the social classes have no time available to represent themselves or to study the issues being debated. Secret clubs and block voting are difficult to combat and also do not lead to decisions of the most benefit to all. At its most pure, direct democracy is mob rule, or governance by decree. This system will allow the mob to override the decisions of constitutions and law, and does not allow for a reliable and consistent social contract for all members of society. In this form, it is hard to argue that direct democracy is even a system of governance at all. Governance by decree is governance

Governance by decree is governance by whim and not just or fair governance under most definitions of the words.

by whim, and not just or fair governance under most definitions of the words. If an individual is to enter a binding social contract with a society, it is essential that they see and can rely on the constitution of the society they are contracting with.

Direct democracy is very popular currently as an alternative to the more widely attempted, and therefore more obviously failed, representative democracy. The Pirate Party uses liquid democracy as an idea to tie votes to expertise and incorporate some aspects of direct democracy within a representative system. This is a recycled idea from historical democracy that was replaced for a reason. Before secret ballots and one vote per person became the norm, people were regularly intimidated out of their votes by tyrannical spouses, employers, or others in a position of power. Liquid democracy is not a new system. It is a return to a previously failed system. It allows both an accepted rule by demagogues and a fertile ground for corruption, vote buying, and intimidation. These are things that were fought and exorcised in earlier times. There is no logical reason to expect a different result from a system that has been tried. Women and the economically disadvantaged fought far too hard to overcome this system to allow it to return.

Chapter 4

Representative Democracy

Representative democracy evolved as a means to overcome some of the obvious flaws of direct democracy. Representative democracy has become a cripplingly paradoxical system which celebrates nouns over verbs and is far more concerned with representation of every conceivable group than the governing actions being taken. The result is a system where individual rights are negotiable, bigotry is integral and action is carried forth with no public debate. Representative democracy is designed not to care about individual rights but to care about what noun each person can identify with and how strong is the lobby group associated with that noun. Representative democracy is divisive, ineffectual and based on impossible principles.

There are two underlying concepts which must be universally accepted for representative democracy to function: groups may act as individuals and individuals may act as groups. These two ideas are fundamentally unsound. While these contradictions were required in earlier attempts at representative governance, the idea was always flawed and recognized as being flawed. As we have progressed to the point where we can eliminate these weaknesses, we have instead greatly increased their use and stopped questioning their appropriateness. Presently, these two concepts contribute to fundamental paradoxes throughout the current system which can only be remedied by rejection of the underlying concepts.

A group is a collection of individuals united for a certain time and space by a specific idea, experience or other common bond. Individuals have the ability to associate, to exchange ideas, to agree, to cooperate, cohabit and in any other way to collaborate, but the group they form does not become an individual. It cannot logically be granted a voice, a vote, or political or legal power. It is only in a system governed by groups and one which does not respect individual rights that such power seems essential.

Conversely, there is never a need for an individual to act as a group. We no longer live in a world where one individual has to make a long arduous journey to appear in person to represent their town or region. We need to work to ensure there is no reason why individuals cannot represent themselves in any circumstance. If the members not speaking are not interested, then they should not participate instead of lending excess weight to another voice. If they are interested but do not understand, the system needs to be changed to allow for ease of understanding, probably by use of concentric user groups and knowledge bridges. If individual voices cause too much noise, the system needs to be modified to provide a solution. Individual voices are to be treasured, not lost for expedience.

An individual speaking for a group is a dishonest mask for an unfairly weighted individual voice in almost every circumstance.

If an individual represents a group, we must ask: Who will have the right to represent the group? What will they be allowed to say? What will the wording be? If any member of the group disagrees, if any word is not approved, then the person speaking for the group is no longer representing the group. That person is now speaking as an individual with words unfairly weighted by group affiliation. The individuals in the represented group who allowed this are equally guilty of misrepresenting themselves as being part of a voice they failed to approve. An individual speaking for a group is a dishonest mask for an unfairly weighted individual voice in almost every circumstance.

When individuals speak as groups, we frequently do not even know who the members behind the groups are, or what their individual opinions are. In many cases, the group is just the voice of one, sometimes a person who speaks, votes, exercises political and legal power and obtains money or other rewards through many different groups. The group names encourage the public to attach undue authority to an individual voice, to think they are donating time, money or effort to a cause for many which benefits only one, and to fail to question the background or connections of an individual they do not see.

Representative democracy is very personality driven. A charismatic leader is given authority seldom commensurate with any expertise or experience. Where the representative falls short in knowledge or experience, they then have the authority to hire the needed expertise, providing a perfectly fertile ground for corruption and cronyism, as well as incompetence. The representatives are assumed to carry all of the attributes and values associated with the group and given trust and blame not earned by themselves. The task of representing others is impossible and perilous in actuality, so the job is rarely taken up by anyone except as an opportunity to further a personal agenda.

It is understood by all that groups and individuals are different entity types with different attributes. The idea that the two may have their attributes exchanged for expedience is no longer expedient. Corporatist groups contribute to an extraordinary degree to the most problematic aspects of current governance, starting with the ones illustrated here and escalating into legal corporate personhood and democratic dictatorships. In order to create a system without the same failings, these two concepts must be rejected as part of the design. Individuals must begin to communicate as ideas and actions, not nouns. Groups must be given only those attributes which are logical to them, such as the ability to assemble.

**Voices, votes, legal and political power
are natural rights of individuals, not groups.**

Chapter 5

Hidden Oligarchies

In *The Iron Law of Oligarchy,* **Robert Michels** holds that any political system eventually devolves into an oligarchy[2]. Representative democracy is the most dishonest oligarchy of all as it insists on the falsehood that the voice of its oligarchs is the voice of the people and the subsequent falsehood that their rule is rule by the people. Democracies have not eradicated oligarchy; they have driven it to secrecy, a state of affairs ironically most abhorrent in a democracy. Instead of confronting the problems inherent in an oligarchy, democracy denies it exists while practicing it openly. Oligarchy is not necessary, but it can only be overcome in a completely open and transparent system which allows the most widespread participation by all, and knowledge for all, and recognizes and accommodates expertise and greater levels of knowledge.

Communist states have failed for the same reasons, by denying and pretending to eradicate elitism instead of acknowledging it and using it to the advantage of society. Many advocates of both democracy and communism hold that their ideas have never been properly tried. The refusal to recognize and control the causes of oligarchies is the reason the concepts behind both will never be implemented despite widespread attempts. These ideologies fail at the gate because of a fatal flaw. When a round peg does not fit in a square hole despite numerous attempts, we do not say it has not been tried, we say it doesn't work.

Representative democracies do not provide for expertise in governance as representatives are elected by land mass and time span, not system, and are usually elected for charisma, not expertise. Athenian sortition likewise made no attempt at combining expertise with authority. Subjects that the majority is unqualified to speak on are delegated to similarly unqualified political representatives, segregated from other representatives by land mass. These representatives appoint experts who obtain their positions by cronyism with the politician instead of expertise acknowledged by the entire interested population.

The politicians and experts in the current system then provide for no meaningful feedback from users of the system, outside of occasional polls. These polls are conducted on test populations which another group have decided shall be considered representative of the population as a whole, and used to provide input on only the questions the experts decide. There is no transparency of any meaningful kind that would allow users of the system to audit what the experts are doing.

We can do better than this. We can govern by user groups, respect individual rights and global commons, and collaborate using stigmergy. We can belong to overlapping societies voluntarily by acceptance of social contracts. Where necessary, elite expertise can be contained and used through transparent epistemic communities with knowledge bridges while control remains with the user group.

Group affiliation

.

Chapter 6

All organized groups of affiliated people are dedicated to promoting the interests of their group members. Unlike individuals, who have the power to change their minds and allegiances at will, or to act outside their own best interests, an organization has a mandate to promote a specific idea and represent a specific group. If an organization were to fail to promote its mandate and population above all others, it would be acting contrary to its reason for existence. The first goal of nation states is to defend their citizens against the 'other', an idea which has led, and will continue to lead, to divisive politics and human rights violations.

People in systems of corporatist groups are proud to identify themselves as members of various groups instead of by their own actions. Anyone proud to self identify as a member of a group is at best a bore. At worst, group affiliation allows them to circumvent personal responsibility and demonize 'outsiders'. A corporatist group has no place in a consensus based system which respects all of its individual participants equally. Individuals who identify as members of a group are frequently less interested in the topic than in the social aspect of being in solidarity with their peers. Groupthink is not only a waste of potentially valuable contributions, it can allow flawed initiatives to pass simply because no one wishes to raise an objection, either the people who wish to maintain their membership in a group or the people who are too intimidated to disagree with them.

In a system where groups representing individuals is the norm, as in the current representative political systems, there is a chronic problem of ensuring representation of all minority groups and hearing their rights alongside other larger groups. The issue is not solved by having more and louder minority groups, in every conceivable combination, making futile attempts to ensure that every group has a seat at every table and designing amplification algorithms for their voices. It is solved by ridding ourselves of all groups speaking as individuals and letting every individual speak for themselves. If individual rights for everyone are put above any group consensus, are a given in every assembly, if they are applied equally without distinction of any kind, there is no need for anyone to have group representation. The completely incongruous situation we have found ourselves in under the current system, where groups demand, and sometimes obtain, special 'individual' rights, would be unnecessary. No group can properly represent the diversity of its members, only the individuals can.

There is no occasion for group endorsements or condemnations of anything when the individuals have their own voices. Both condemnations and endorsements encourage what ought to be assemblies of individuals with equal voices to place undue importance on pleasing the individuals belonging to the opposing or endorsing group. Dissenting voices from the group are not represented, and individual nuance is lost.

Group affiliation behind individual voices allows listeners to reject ideas before hearing them. Labeling an idea as coming from The Left or The Right is enough for many people to refuse to listen to it at all. Other equally irrelevant group affiliations result in equally damaging bigotry which prevents communication on any topic. In a system which is built on communication and consensus, such barriers are insupportable.

Group representation of individuals contributes to the infantilization of the individuals and allows them to relax and not educate themselves or take part in their own governance. Corporatist groups are fundamental to all centralized and totalitarian government systems, and antithetical to all open and consensual governance. Corporatist groups produce the same effect locally as they do nationally and globally. The cells create the whole; corporatist groups can never create a consensual system. It is impossible to reconcile corporatist thinking at any level with an open system of communication and governance. A structure like the United Nations reaching consensus is far removed from a real global consensus.

Group affiliation is essential for the dehumanization of 'others' required for systemic violation of the human rights of a group. Group affiliation encourages pride in whatever noun people identify as, instead of what actions they have taken. This is the root of all racism, nationalism, ageism, sexism, and every other form of bigotry.

Increasingly, people around the world are being jailed for being nouns, or affiliated with nouns, instead of for any action they have taken.

Group affiliation is never necessary to call out discrimination. Instead of embracing feminism, the world needs to call out masculinism. It is masculinism that keeps men in positions of privilege, and it is rejecting masculinism that will create change. Promoting feminism creates a power struggle with masculinism and leaves minorities such as transgendered people still fighting for their rights. Rejecting all the -ism's brings equality.

It is recognized worldwide that criminal actions are what people are tried in a court of law and jailed for. Increasingly, people around the world are being jailed for being nouns, or affiliated with nouns, instead of for any action they have taken. People are called 'illegal' and put in jail without having taken any action at all. Sometimes, they are accused of illegal entry into a country, which is an action but only a crime for members of certain groups. At other times, people are declared illegal even in the country of their birth where they cannot even be accused of illegal entry.

People are also accused and imprisoned for being affiliated with nouns as shown in the infamous 'anti-terrorism' laws enacted around the world. Under these laws, anyone from a taxi driver to a journalist can be imprisoned simply by sticking 'al Qaeda' in front of their action[3]. Even if they are only a child, they can be accused of being 'al Qaeda royalty' and imprisoned without trial or assassinated. Identical actions are condemned or justified depending on whether it is the group identified as 'good guys' or 'bad guys' doing it. Collective punishment, recognized as a war crime in the fourth Geneva Convention, is accepted in the form of sanctions when it is endorsed by the United Nations. The same action by a weak state would be considered genocidal, as it is.

Collective privilege and collective punishment are only possible through group affiliation. Groups without privilege can be made career victims by having NGO's created to represent them. NGOs set up to combat rape against women turn away and *i*gnore male victims[4] as they are looking for defined victim groups, not fighting actions. Groups identified as victims are turned into products for lobby groups and fundraisers. Once a group becomes a product, the interest is in differentiating them further to enhance the need for their representation. Western pundits can yawn over the deaths of slave workers in another country as slavery works best 'for them' and prevents further hardship on 'our own poor'[5]. These concepts are not possible without group affiliation to identify who 'they' and 'we' are.

The single greatest tool for making moral people commit atrocities is group affiliation. The single greatest tool for promoting global human rights and equality is to end group affiliation.

Natural and negotiated rights

Chapter 7

"The only purpose for which power can be rightfully exercised over any member of a civilized community, against his will, is to prevent harm to others." - John Stuart Mill and Harriet Taylor, *On Liberty*[6]

"Liberty consists in the freedom to do everything which injures no one else; hence the exercise of the natural rights of each man has no limits except those which assure to the other members of the society the enjoyment of the same rights." - *Declaration of the Rights of Man and of the Citizen*[7]

Individual rights must be the first goal of every society and inherent in every system. As unhealthy cells can never create a healthy whole, a weakened people stripped of their basic rights will never create a healthy society. In any system where groups have power, individual rights are always at risk. Both democracy and communism have brought human rights horrors every bit as reprehensible as fascist states. In order to guard against genocide, torture, and other persecution of individuals in the name of the greater good, a society must safeguard individual rights above all other authority.

In order for any society to ensure its survival without the use of tyrannical force, the members must be convinced that it is better than the alternative. If an alternative, or no society at all, appears more attractive than the current state, people will naturally be motivated to dismantle the current system. In order for a society to appear more attractive than no society at all, we need to consider the basic rights of individuals in no society. There are certain basic rights that we can see enjoyed by most mammals in their natural state. To ensure that people do not need to resort to fighting for these basic rights, we can enshrine them in our social contract. If people can see their basic rights more attainable within the system than without, it will be in their best interests to protect the system.

Every undomesticated mammal will seek and sometimes fight for their basic needs: food, shelter, safety, the right to reproduce and to provide for and educate their young, the right to cohabit, at least with offspring, some measure of privacy, the right to associate or refuse to associate, the right to communicate, the right to explore and the right to learn. To some extent, all mammals have also the right to choose the time, place and method of their work within the bounds of nature and survival.

Any interference with these basic rights is seen as an attack and will greeted with whatever defence the mammal is capable of.

If an individual agrees to abide by the laws of a society and not attack it, it is reasonable that the society provides means for all members to attain the same advantages they would fight for in a state of nature. When a society refuses to allow its members to attain basic needs such as food, shelter and safety, and the deprivation is not caused by unavailability, only the most extreme repressive force and mass imprisonment will protect the society from revolution.

We do not have human dignity in a system where our basic needs are treated not as a right but as a privilege.

Given access to basic needs, the commonly recognized advantage undomesticated mammals have which their domesticated counterparts do not is freedom. Domesticated mammals are widely recognized as being in some sort of slavery, though it is popular lately to equate their status to a permanently infantilized 'member of the family' instead, unless they are destined to be eaten. In either case, they do not have the free will they would have in a state of nature. They will never attain an adult, autonomous status or the dignity of self actualization.

When speaking of both domesticated animals and humans, many people question why they would even want free will. They are, after all, completely taken care of, subject of course to the whims of their masters. Given proper laws to ensure benevolent masters, what is so bad about slavery or perpetual childhood? The idea that we are all entitled to our human dignity is perhaps more easily understood. We do not have human dignity when we lose, not just our basic rights to survival, but also our free will and our right to reach our full potential. We do not have human dignity when we are not treated as responsible, intelligent, participating members of society. We do not have human dignity when we are kept in a state below what we are capable of achieving or in a system which fails to recognize where we naturally excel. And we do not have human dignity in a system where our basic needs are treated not as a right but as a privilege which we must earn and be grateful for and which a higher parental authority can remove from us.

It has become a common and accepted part of society that when people reach an age where they ought to have attained adulthood, they frequently express 'unreasonable' dissatisfaction, in the form of riots or other violence against their society. Where a socioeconomic excuse for this behaviour can be found, this will be commonly used by sociologists to justify the incidents, but when the perpetrators come from the most advantaged segments of society, puzzlement and frustration are the response. Rebellion is completely expected by childhood development experts when caregivers refuse to allow a child the independence required for them to attain adulthood. It is curious that the same expectation is not attached to a society that refuses to allow people to attain adult status and responsibility.

Current political systems around the world typically discuss individual rights from the role of either a 'good' parent or 'bad' parent. The harsh parent will argue that individuals must bear full responsibility for all that happens to them, in the form of severe punishment for infractions of rules and no aid in times of need. The benevolent parent will argue for all encompassing care for each member of society. Neither argues for individual rights that would give not just responsibility but also authority to the people, as this would eliminate the political systems as they exist today.

The rights which all individuals in a society are entitled to are typically enshrined in a constitutional or human rights agreement at a national or international level. Because these agreements are most often produced at times following revolution, newly won independence, or other periods of great awareness, they tend to reflect the ideals of the people in the society. They frequently include life, liberty, security of person, access to the basic essentials of life including knowledge, privacy and personal autonomy in matters not affecting the rest of society, free development of personality and potential, and an unbiased and accessible legal system which does not promote the wishes of the group over the rights of the individual. The rights in these documents form the social contract between individuals and society. Each individual agrees that they will work for the greater good of the society and protect the individual rights of others in exchange for having their own rights protected. This contract is essential in a system of governance that is not simply mob rule, or despotic rule.

If a governing authority were to pass laws in contradiction to the social contract, the government would be in breach of contract. The people in the society can then remove the authority given to the government or consider the contract null and void and declare a state of no governance from which a new social contact may or may not be formed. The governing body loses authority when it acts in contradiction to the social contract. A ruling such as that in the Supreme Court of Canada, which found that the government of Canada had violated the Charter of Rights and Freedoms in the case of Guantanamo detainee Omar Khadr and yet left the government with the authority to decide the remedy, while legally justifiable under current Canadian law, is logically incorrect.

If mob rule is allowed to change the social contract to remove rights from individuals in the name of the greater good, the social contract with each member of society is also null and void. If the point of a social contract is that each individual agrees that they will work for the greater good of the society and protect the individual rights of others in exchange for having their own rights protected, every violation of anyone's rights needs to be of grave concern to the whole of society. The greater good has never and will never be served by laws which violate individual rights for the benefit of overall society.

Almost every law which violates a social contract is brought in as a one time exception that will only violate the rights of a certain minority group and will only apply in one or very few scenarios. It is usually presented as a protection of the rights of a highly sympathetic group with majority approval and accompanied by demonization of the target minority group. Sweeping surveillance of the internet is marketed as protecting children from predators and allowing law enforcement to prevent child rape and torture media, despite all evidence that it does nothing of the kind and is not actually intended to. Internet users are depicted as potential child predators and pirates of copyrighted material, particularly if they have privacy concerns or fight against censorship. Removal of citizenship of Rohingya Muslims in Burma, the United States Patriot Act which criminalized providing expert advice or assistance (including legal) to designated terrorists, the massive worldwide loss of rights and liberty, not to mention life, in the name of 'counter terrorism', the 'state of emergency' invoked around the world at various times which, once invoked, frequently becomes a permanent state: it is very easy to find countless examples of rights violations in current law. In every instance above, these governments have broken their social contract. They have become coercive societies which now must rule by force.

These sweeping changes are usually preceded by creeping changes felt only by the marginalized in society and frequently billed as 'for their own good'. Various laws and regulations in both Canada and the Netherlands which endanger people by restricting legal prostitution in ways that would not be tolerated in other legal careers are an example. In practice, the marginalized members of any society seldom enjoy the rights that form society's contract with them. Until every member of society makes it their business to defend the rights of every other member of society, no society will be safe from these encroachments.

If the marginalized group can be given a group name, anything from 'Palestinians' to 'terrorists' to 'Anonymous', the success of the violation of their rights is far more likely. If the majority of the population does not identify as part of the victimized group they are easily able to accept the loss of rights, especially if it is accompanied by propaganda to villainize the group. In this case, the entire society has broken their social contract and the society has lost legitimacy.

In the United States this concept of villainized 'other' was carried to the entire rest of the world in the Patriot Act. It was not until the government passed legislation in the form of the 2012 NDAA, which attempted to treat US citizens in the same manner that the entire rest of the world were treated, that the US public became outraged. This followed ten years of apathy over Guantanamo Bay and other secret prisons worldwide which continues today. Such an extreme case suggests a strong need for a worldwide social contract which tolerates no 'others', particularly as states put defence of their citizens as their first priority. It is easy from there to justify defending citizens, not by supporting them, but instead by persecuting others. Individual rights must apply to every individual, and every law, including those of borders and nationality, which differentiates between groups will undermine individual rights.

Chapter 8

Human Rights Law

Currently, the world has not fought for individual human rights in large numbers since the end of World War II which left us with the Universal Declaration of Human Rights [8]. Those rights have been largely eroded, unnoticed by most of the world. Historically, a lack of awareness of violations to social contracts was both real and excusable, and the ability to organize in protest was severely hampered. That is no longer the case.

Since the UDHR was written in 1948, it has been under relentless attack, as has every other documentation of rights before or since. Although the preamble clearly states the intent to *"strive by teaching and education to promote respect for these rights and freedoms and by progressive measures, national and international, to secure their universal and effective recognition and observance, both among the peoples of Member States themselves and among the peoples of territories under their jurisdiction"* the text, widely distributed in early years, is now rarely seen. The Covenants adopted in 1966, law since 1976, billed as 'clarifying the UDHR' and written in far more convoluted terms, are one of the first significant examples of legal undermining which, if the principles of the UDHR had been followed, would never have passed.

For example:

UDHR Article 3.

Everyone has the right to life, liberty and security of person.

Article 3 was completely negated by the Covenants, which start by adding the word 'arbitrarily', and then proceed to remove the right to life from everyone not under 18 or pregnant. (Even this was disregarded by the law in several countries, most notably the United States.):

International Covenant on Civil and Political Rights Article 6.[9]

1. Every human being has the inherent right to life. This right shall be protected by law. No one shall be arbitrarily deprived of his life.

2. In countries which have not abolished the death penalty, sentence of death may be imposed only for the most serious crimes in accordance with the law in force at the time of the commission of the crime and not contrary to the provisions of the present Covenant and to the Convention on the Prevention and Punishment of the Crime of Genocide. This penalty can only be carried out pursuant to a final judgment rendered by a competent court.

5. Sentence of death shall not be imposed for crimes committed by persons below eighteen years of age and shall not be carried out on pregnant women.

UDHR Article 4:

No one shall be held in slavery or servitude; slavery and the slave trade shall be prohibited in all their forms.

This was modified to separate "forced or compulsory labour" as somehow different from "slavery or servitude" and allow prison labour, which has since become a thriving slave industry. It also includes enough vague generality to be very flexible in allowing any form of state slavery.

International Covenant on Civil and Political Rights

Article 8:

1. No one shall be held in slavery; slavery and the slave-trade in all their forms shall be prohibited.

2. No one shall be held in servitude.

3. (a) No one shall be required to perform forced or compulsory labour;

(b) Paragraph 3 (a) shall not be held to preclude, in countries where imprisonment with hard labour may be imposed as a punishment for a crime, the performance of hard labour in pursuance of a sentence to such punishment by a competent court;

(c) For the purpose of this paragraph the term "forced or compulsory labour" shall not include:

(i) Any work or service, not referred to in subparagraph (b), normally required of a person who is under detention in consequence of a lawful order of a court, or of a person during conditional release from such detention;

(ii) Any service of a military character and, in countries where conscientious objection is recognized, any national service required by law of conscientious objectors;

(iii) Any service exacted in cases of emergency or calamity threatening the life or well-being of the community;

(iv) Any work or service which forms part of normal civil obligations.

In case there was anything left of the UDHR that may hinder a state from doing exactly as they please, it is made clear that the state may limit any of these rights *"solely for the purpose of promoting the general welfare in a democratic society"* which instantly renders the entire body of human rights law null and void.

International Covenant on Economic, Social and Cultural Rights Article 4 [10]

The States Parties to the present Covenant recognize that, in the enjoyment of those rights provided by the State in conformity with the present Covenant, the State may subject such rights only to such limitations as are determined by law only in so far as this may be compatible with the nature of these rights and solely for the purpose of promoting the general welfare in a democratic society.

Chapter 9

Building a new society

Reading the thirty UDHR articles is highly recommended. Most people today are suspicious, and rightly so, of any document from the United Nations, but this was the first document and, as a product of its time, it is shockingly complete and beautiful in its simplicity. That is not to argue that it does not need an update, but most of the updates suggested in the past detract by addition. The UDHR, while very improvable, is a model of how principles ought to be written, in simple, pure and universal terms upon which law can be based, with no vague flowery generalities that require interpretation.

The idea that only a lawyer can understand the law was created to disguise the undermining of the basic principles of society. In order for a social contract to be binding, the principles must be easily taught to anyone, including children. No law must ever deviate from the principles of the social contract, therefore law ought to be largely intuitive. It is evident from the above that a vigilant society must audit, and indeed write, all new laws to prevent the undermining of principles.

Along with accessibility of the law, the inviolability of principles has also been under attack. A very short time ago (when the UDHR was written), principles were considered the foundation's upon which everything must be built, as they are in every science and discipline. If someone said they were against your idea in principle, your task of convincing them became far harder. You must now first convince them that either your argument fit their principle, or their principle was wrong. If you succeeded at the latter, that person would have to rethink their values on everything, because morals and values were to be built upon core principles, as was the law. Today, if a politician says they are against something in principle, it means they have already agreed. Principles have been designated as niceties that we all appreciate in theory but are impractical. This is an Orwellian attack on the structure of a society which clears the path for every oxymoronic law which has followed.

In order to stop the incessant flow of laws against the will of the people, core principles of society must be defined. When these principles are defined, it must be recognized that no law can ever be passed which contradicts these principles. In order for society to be stable without representation and allow a new and better system of collaboration, principles must apply equally to everyone, without exception.

The law must be accessible for all, not only the wealthy. Currently, NGO's are required to fight for the rights of people and nature, but corporate rights are protected by their access to the expensive legal system. Legal remedies must be as immediate as possible as powerful interests can destroy lives just as surely be protracting a court case as they can by winning one. The law must be intuitive, not up to the subjective judgment of an archaic legal system. Members of a society need to know before committing an act what the repercussions of that act will be, and the law must be applied equally to all. This requires a far more automated and accessible system than is currently available in any country. The fact that the legal system has remained so archaic strongly suggests that it is meant to remain inaccessible and subjective as that is best serving the interests of those in power.

The discouragement people once faced for obtaining online medical advice, particularly from their peers, is greatly compounded for legal advice. This must change. People must recreate the legal systems to work for them, and that requires direct involvement at every level in the creation and implementation of the laws. The law, more than any other part of society, must be transparent, accessible, equal, and created by and for the people.

Heather Marsh

Society vs dissociation

Chapter 10

The last chapter talked of a state of nature where society did not exist. In truth, such a state has never existed outside of social contract theory because humans are social animals and we have always created societies. In today's structure, society with its dependencies and relationships has been converted to a completely monetized system of dissociation. For the first time in human history, people have been effectively dissociated from each other and are living in a state of no society. Humans are social animals. We want a society. Humans also want dignity, including the right to attain adulthood and achieve our full potential. Both of these are biological needs hard coded into humans and we feel deep unrest at their removal.

Figure 1: Leeches and basic needs

In the illustration above, all of people's basic needs are enclosed in the top space. This can include food, housing, health care, education, lifework, and even family. These essential resources are separated from the people and held in a space not accessible to them. If the resource is health care, a member of the public is not able to review the work of the health professionals. They do not have access to pharmaceutical studies, cannot choose the remedy they wish, and cannot assist others. All resources are funneled through the authoritative organizations, called leeches. A leech is a parasite that attaches itself to a host and drains the host while contributing nothing. In society, our leeches are financial institutions, old style media institutions (the ones internal to each system as well as public broadcasters), regulatory bodies, training and licensing institutions, distributors of goods and services and all other bodies set up to regulate the flow of resources to the society. None of these leeches contribute to society. They simply control access to resources.

> **Every conceivable resource has had access removed from the society and placed in the control of leeches.**

In the food system, duty, trade restrictions and trade treaties control access to food. Government regulatory bodies control both production and distribution, even preventing food sharing between people or scavenging from waste food (for example by requiring chlorine bleach to be poured over food in dumpsters). In the education system, the universities control who can learn, control their learning, and produce a credential that allows a person to perform work. The freedom to learn and the power of peer promotion is removed to an outside regulatory body in almost every profession. In science and art, intellectual property laws prevent collaboration, study and use of prior work and encourage secrecy and information hoarding. Even sport (games) and entertainment are strictly controlled and regulated by bylaws, causing both to be largely replaced by professional organizations with access funneled through leeches. Every conceivable resource has had access removed from the society and placed in the control of leeches.

This system of dissociation is so entrenched in society that it is very seldom questioned. Money for health care is equated to money for insurance, even though insurance companies do not provide health care. Banks need to be propped up to provide housing, even though banks do not provide housing. The almighty economy must be saved even at the cost of untold lives, or life on earth itself, but we can't eat the economy. Education and information are controlled, not produced, by existing institutions. Both could and should be provided by transparency and open access. Distributors should be replaced by farm-gate importing, information wants and needs to be free, and choosing one's own lifework is a basic right not to be removed by regulatory bodies.

In this system of dissociation, individuals have no societal protection. Each is dangling from the leech by their own little vein with a limited access to resources. There are no direct relationships or dependencies. Even if the access allows the person plentiful amounts of everything, there is a built in awareness of shortage and reliance on the system that strongly discourages sharing. If one person's vein is broken, their need is met by hostility from the others dangling by their own veins. To rescue another is to weaken oneself. Predictably, rescuing those in need requires the creation of more leeches in the form of NGOs and government regulatory bodies for people in crisis. This results in a transference of responsibility that prevents society as a whole from spending much time considering those who their society fails. All the NGOs and regulatory bodies do is distribute and control the generosity from the rest of society (and take a very large cut for themselves) but people are conditioned to believe the NGOs actually provide the support.

Ironically, the individuals whose access to the leech is for some reason broken are referred to themselves as leeches. The Tax Payer was invented to assert moral control over other members of society such as children, anyone in crisis, prisoners and anyone who dares to work outside a corporate approved role. The Tax Payer is encouraged by relentless propaganda and enabled by the financial system to consider themselves both the backbone of society, as evidenced on monetary flowcharts and nowhere else, and personally robbed by all others. When people look for the source of the obvious flaws in the systems of dissociation, they are always pointed to those that are not acting as The Tax Payer. Seldom does society look past the propaganda to the real leeches.

Original society is formed by a mother giving birth to a child. Once a mother becomes pregnant, dependency has been created and she must surround herself with a support network, or a society. At the very least, if her society is to survive, she must create a support network between herself and her child or find another caretaker for her child. A mother and a child is the basic unit of a society, a unit with dependencies and unequal ability working for a common goal. This is where a new society must start to plan a new direction. There are many dependencies in a full society besides children. Children are the original core, because without them a society dies, but a full society will also have people with a variety of mental and physical limitations and gifts. In today's un-society people with any dependencies are seen as worthless, or at best inferior, instead of different. Today's ideal is a young, healthy, intelligent adult with no dependencies.

In today's un-society, the core element has been two or more men shaking hands. That is not a society, that is a trade relationship. The fallacy of equality for women is dependent on their simulation of that ideal. Women are offered an equal opportunity to participate in trade relationships. A trade relationship must occur among equally advantaged partners if one is not to be taken at a disadvantage. Dependencies are abhorrent in a trade relationship. Dependencies and sharing weaken a trading partner; ownership strengthens them.

Figure 2: True society

A true society is shown in the previous diagram which is starting to manifest in various forms around the world (and still exists in a very few). In it, every society includes the entire user group and no one but the user group. No one outside the user group can control the activity inside. Access is restricted for none. Information is available to all through transparency. Education is available to all from their peers, and through epistemic communities with knowledge bridges. Anyone can submit work through concentric user groups or stigmergy.

Radical privacy and radical transparency

Chapter 11

I t is essential for participatory government that organizations which affect the public be transparent to the public. Without full information, people are incapable of making the decisions required to participate in their own governance. In the past, any secrets by public organizations, short of war secrets, were grounds for a scandal. A free media and freedom of speech were considered essential in a democracy so that transparency of public matters could be ensured.

Today, the public has to prove why it needs to know any information about its government and go through an expensive and labour intensive process to acquire information that will arrive, if it arrives at all, after great delay and in a very censored form. Information on corporations is simply unattainable except by illegal methods as corporations, which include prison, intelligence, military, pharmaceutical, agricultural, and even police agencies, are considered private. These private corporations now own rights to global commons such as our oceans, space and electromagnetic field, as well as the individual environments of each of us.

A huge industry has built up around filtering, hoarding, spinning and occasionally doling out to the public in innocuous bits without context, all information about organizations and actions which effect the public. The true information that reaches the public is more than drowned out by the equally huge industry of misinformation being produced and distributed by the same public organizations. Our media exists to convince us that our right to information is actually a right to know whether an arbitrarily selected private citizen has had a haircut instead of a right to the information we need in order to govern ourselves.

Another massive industry exists to gather, store, analyze and distribute every conceivable detail of private information on private citizens. Corporations gather and store information on every aspect of individual lives and make it available to any organization with the finances or skill to retrieve it. There is no discrimination in what is gathered as organizations have decided that any private information is an unknown unknown. They may just not know if they need it or not, so they need it all. Legal changes and popular propaganda have created such oxymoronic beasts as public individuals and private corporations to cause confusion over these very clear violations of the two basic principles.

There is no such thing as a private organization, outside of purely social groups. There is no such thing as a public person, only public actions by private individuals.

Under the current system, even when people become convinced of the soundness of the principles of privacy for individuals and transparency for organizations and actions which affect the public, they advocate a modified version of this rule as reasonable, the result of compromise and good sense, and not radical like a whole hearted embrace of the principles would be. They point to many situations where the principles in pure form simply would not work. Principles however, if they are sound at all, must work in all cases. If they do not, there is a fault either with the principle, or the case. The answer in our current society has been to reject the principles as nice ideas which we will keep in our legal foundations but ignore in reality as they are simply not practical. A more accurate answer may be found by looking at the cases where these two principles appear to produce poor results.

The release of the US state cables was widely condemned because of the release of the names of private individuals who were providing information to public organizations. The exposure of any private individual to harm must be regarded as an ill. But if harm was caused, it was caused not by the action which abided by the principles but by the earlier actions in violation of the principles. The individuals in question had a right to privacy. Why were their names recorded and placed in an extremely public and easy to access database? Why were their names recorded at all? Why did those individuals need to make secret reports about public organizations or actions to other public organizations? If the principle regarding public organizations and actions was followed, there would be no need for informants. If the principle regarding privacy for individuals was followed, the names would never have been recorded.

Another case frequently brought forward is the harm to individuals by criminals such as drug cartels in South America if the cartels knew about individuals who are reporting them. Under the current system, they already know, as do the state cable informant's enemies. Once information about an individual is stored, the principle of individual privacy which ought to protect that person has been ignored, leaving them completely exposed. Again, that individual ought also to be protected by the principle of transparency for public organizations. If the entire country was working together in a structure that allowed them to expose all actions of the drug cartels, the individuals would not need to be put at risk. If we apply the two principles from the beginning, they work in every hazardous situation.

Law enforcement and military around the world have claimed the right to operate in complete secrecy as that is the only way to catch 'the bad guys'. Transparency would enable the public to catch the bad guys on both sides. A public that was involved in helping to enforce laws could accomplish far more than a police force could by itself. Instead of blocking the entire internet under the pretense of blocking child rape and torture media sites, the police could just ask or allow the public to police the internet. If child rape and torture media or terrorist plotting sites can be found by anyone, they can be found by everyone. What is required is not secrecy and censorship but a proper structure for policing which involves the public. The only cases in which this would not work is when the law is not one the public agrees with, which is a great method of providing feedback that the law needs to be modified to represent the people more accurately.

Diplomats and others in positions of power have complained that transparency makes it difficult for them to do their jobs. Where that is the case, the fault must be found with their jobs. The current system is a massive, tangled tortuous mess of spies, media, spokespeople, communication departments, freedom of information laws and lobbies, actions and counteractions attempting to maintain balance in a system which preaches democracy and practices totalitarianism. The difficulty and confusion is caused by the current system, not the proposed one. Entire industries would be made redundant by adherence to the principle of transparency for public organizations. Transparency is needed, not selected pieces of isolated information wrapped up and presented by an official but full transparency, of the kind that would allow any passerby to see exactly what an organization was up to. As the current powers have been asking private individuals for decades, what do they have to hide?

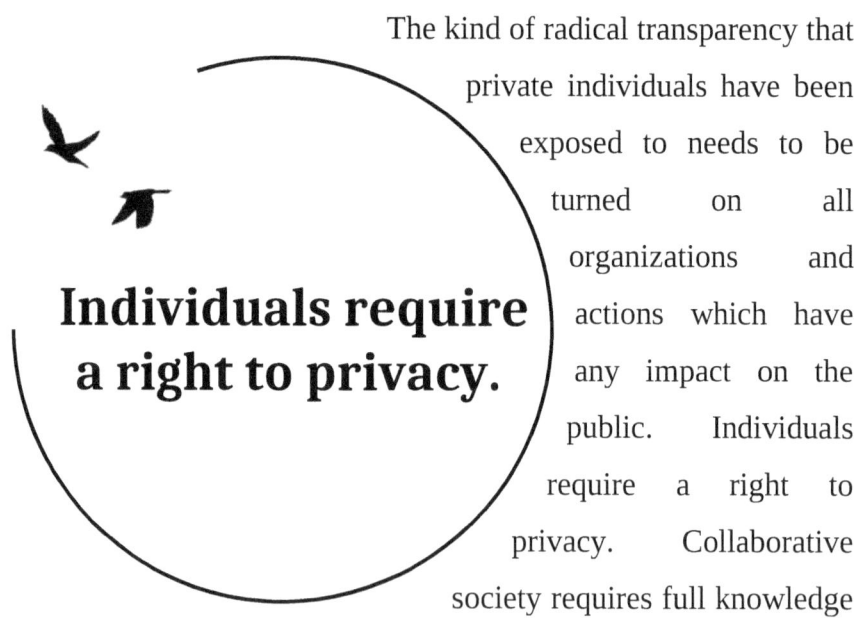

The kind of radical transparency that private individuals have been exposed to needs to be turned on all organizations and actions which have any impact on the public. Individuals require a right to privacy. Collaborative society requires full knowledge of organizations and actions which affect the public.

Individuals require a right to privacy.

In the past, most of the world acknowledged, in both cultural norms and the law, that privacy was a basic individual right. It could be argued that this right was ours in a state of nature. Mammals in general do keep personal matters private to varying degrees, and privacy can in many cases be equated with personal security. Culturally, it was an accepted practice in many regions of the world that personal business and family business were to be kept private, too much disclosure was frowned upon, and 'snooping' was met with 'mind your own business'. Even names were in many cultures not to be handed out in full to people outside intimate circles, and even within families, personal names were not always used. One of the last vestiges of privacy to be found in western society is that children still frequently do not call their parents by their first names. The rest of the world now does.

In our surveillance culture of today, privacy is again quite literally illegal as it was in previous totalitarian states. 'If you see something say something' and the US FBI's all encompassing 'Suspicious Activity' list have made any attempt at privacy, over even the most innocuous activity, grounds for suspicion of 'terrorism'. The prying of other members of your society is supported by government and corporate surveillance of everything from your conversations and your constantly tracked images to the amount of body heat you are giving off at a 'checkpoint'.

The agenda of the states has been transferred to the wider culture. Now all forms of privacy and even introversion have come to be viewed as negative traits. Anyone who is uncomfortable with sustained eye contact is labeled as hostile or untrustworthy, anyone who works more easily in solitary is 'having trouble integrating' and even the new protest movements embrace all new forms of thinking except solitary. The mainstreaming of privacy invasion makes it almost impossible to avoid having your personal data made available to all, but even if that is managed, your features are available to face recognition, gait recognition, and similar software through surveillance cameras around the world. These are easily matched to all of the rest of your data by the 'two pieces of picture id' required to function in any easy way in modern society.

The normalizing of privacy invasion has spilled over into societies around the world. It is commonplace now for introductions to be followed by what amounts to an interrogation, with all personal and professional background demanded before acquaintance begins. It is even perfectly normal to approach complete strangers with demands to know all of their personal data. This new custom, encouraged by law enforcement in the United States, is endorsed by mainstream society. Any attempt to refuse personal information at first contact is met with indignation. The interrogator, who once would be labeled a 'snoop' is now characterized as 'open', 'honest', and having 'nothing to hide', while the victim is held to be a deviant of some sort or other and regarded with suspicion. The surveillance state has done its job when any request for privacy is met with shock, hurt, accusations of paranoia, and group shunning.

Invasion of the personal lives of individuals has been an accepted feature in the news media for decades. The public's 'right to know', which once applied to the right to know all news required to participate in their own governance, essential in a democracy, became a right to know personal information. All individuals are private individuals; only their actions which affect public life are of public interest. Private individuals were labelled public individuals based on a very arbitrary assignment of all professions 'in the public eye', such as entertainment, as public, The relabelling of these professions was then used to strip basic privacy rights from the professionals. While this was probably started to deflect attention from the matters those in power did not wish attention to be directed towards, and encouraged by celebrities who were profiting from it, the custom has since expanded to include an ever increasing amount of private individuals whose personal lives are in the news for no explicable reason.

As the general population has taken over media gathering and dissemination, the old media's predatory nature has also become dispersed throughout the population. As the old media feels it has the right to use advanced surveillance attacks, stalking and sexual harassment in the form of creep shots, physical mobbing and verbal abuse to any woman who begins to have a voice in society, the internet is now also full of people who feel they are entitled to use the same tactics on any woman or girl who dares to enter the internet public forum. Any woman who attempted to work in news or politics would be met with relentless attacks on her personal life and physical appearance by old media. Any woman who speaks or posts a picture on the internet now is subjected to the same treatment.

A society that has grown up with sexual harassment of women labelled by male dominated media as 'free speech' does not understand this harassment for what it is, mass censorship of female voices. The old media, instead of acknowledging their own behaviour staring back at them from the internet, lobbies against 'cyber bullying', as if what they do is somehow different if it is done online, and claim the solution is for those bullied to lose all possibility of the protection of anonymity.

In order to have a society in which individual needs are respected, a balance must be struck between the right to speak and have freedom of information versus the right to participate equally in society and own the truth about ourselves. Our presentation of ourselves is directly tied to our right to privacy.

People tend to overlook and belittle the impact of privacy violation, primarily as it so often is directed towards those with marginalized voices, but a look at the amount of suicides, as well as mental health problems caused by these violations is enough to show its importance.

The lack of importance placed on privacy may also be directly related to the rule by extroverts we have been subjected to since the beginnings of society. Until we had the internet, the leaders of large crowds were almost always charismatic people with a gift for public speaking and a natural resistance to personal attack through belonging to powerful demographic groups. As the internet has gained in power to the point where it is a direct threat to those currently holding power, as online feedback replaces public shouting matches, the powerful in the molecular world have sought to expose and control those in the online world. Any involuntary exposure has been met by violent reaction from the internet as it is the first place for many that has ever felt like a safe place to speak. One reason Anonymous and the internet in general has had a low opinion of those who seek personal fame may be that the internet is well populated by those who have been persecuted and had their voices repressed by others who easily acquire fame and social power.

The voices of the part of the population who are naturally more introverted, or the almost everyone eliminated from mainstream forums for one reason or another, are at least as important as those currently heard. This however, completely changes the society we are accustomed to, if the voiceless suddenly gain voices, if the creators no longer need the marketers, women do not need to speak through men, and children, the elderly, discriminated minorities, the ostracized of all societies can suddenly speak and have their messages amplified as well as anyone else. This would eliminate huge swathes of industry from communication and representative types of roles, everything from politicians, to media, to marketing companies and NGOs. Not at all coincidentally, all of the lobby groups attempting to control the internet, strip privacy and anonymity, and manage access are from the groups who would no longer be required if everyone had a voice.

Personal information is power. Anyone who can obtain personal information on another has increased their power over the other. That power ought not to be given lightly without established trust. What seems perfectly innocuous until it surfaces as a book, revenge porn, or what ought to be irrelevant attacks on a message by character assassination of the messenger, ought to be kept private by default. Personal information is still every bit as valuable as our grandparents knew it to be. Until and unless our societies mature to the point where we are governed by idea driven instead of personality driven systems, we need to recognize that freedom of speech which is a mask for suppression of the speech of others. When we see private information being used to violate someone's well being, it is no more appropriate to blame the victim for the existence of the information than it is for police in India to assume that if a woman has consensual sex with one man then she can't complain if his friends join in[11].

This is not to argue that we need laws inhibiting privacy violations. We have such laws and they only protect the powerful from exposure of secrets the public needs to know. We need a change in societal attitude, where we no longer applaud or tolerate assaults on privacy, personal attacks on public figures and, most of all, those public invasions of privacy that amount to sexual assault, whether committed by the old media or the internet.

Personal information is power.

Even more than privacy, anonymity is viewed as a hostile act by those in power. A culture in which fame is the ultimate achievement cannot understand the value of ownerless ideas and shapeshifting personas. Anonymity has been equated almost exclusively with criminal activity by politicians and lawmakers.

Online anonymity is cherished by internet dwellers as the only means to pure thought exchange, where ideas can be judged on their own merits, unclouded by preconceived judgements based on unrelated data. Anonymity can be a revelation, as new personas can be tried on and provoke new reactions, revealing our stereotypes and inability to separate messages from messengers.

Anonymity is also simply practical safety. It has been proven enough times that authorities do not need to see any transactions or have evidence of any criminal activity to destroy your life, It is enough that you pull attention, that they are aware of your existence. The fact that you are doing nothing wrong or illegal is no protection if you have attracted the attention of someone with power or mental instability. Governments are not the only people on the internet. If you start expressing opinions you will find far more interesting opposition as well. Anonymity, once lost, can never be regained. Even if you have no intention of ever expressing a controversial opinion, privacy should become a habit, like brushing your teeth.

In many cases, anonymity is the only way for a messenger to ensure their message will be heard. Very often the story of the messenger will override the message. That is the way corporate media has been increasingly covering the news. We are at this point left with only messengers, rarely any message at all, and it is what audiences are trained to look for. Even when choosing political representation, *"I don't like him"* is a perfectly accepted argument. In other cases, the message will be drowned out by the idea that the messenger is an inappropriate source, either because of association or because of who they are[12]. Der Speigel and others lectured members of Pussy Riot on speaking at all when they had young children and the Putin government used their identities to threaten to remove their children. Media subsequently labeled their political message a 'feminist' one, based on nothing at all other than their sex[13].

Pseudonymity is the best of both worlds for many, an identity which allows relationships and trust but also provides control over personal information. This can be essential to create a personality which allows your voice to be heard in the way that you wish it to be. In the future, perhaps we will see everyone with at least three identities: one to carry the two pieces of ID required by the military industrial complex, one for family and friends in molecular life, and one for online idea exchange.

Idea driven systems

Chapter 12

"Turing believes machines think. Turing lies with men. Therefore machines cannot think." – Alan Turing

Representative democracies are part of a personality driven celebrity culture where people are encouraged to support their chosen personalities or groups in any action they take. This has changed from recent history, where celebrity culture existed but was moderated. People were encouraged to choose principles they supported and ensure those principles were met by any action, regardless of the actor. The advantage of a personality driven system to those in power is it allows them to disregard the principles agreed to in a social contract. It also makes favour swapping and influence peddling the preferred methods of negotiation rather than simply negotiating each action on its own merits, a situation apparent in representative governance assemblies such as the United Nations.

When any criticism of an action taken by person A is met by cries that you must then support person B, we are dealing with a personality driven system. When similar actions that make Zimbabwe's President Mugabe an alleged war criminal make the United States President Obama a Nobel Peace Prize winner, we are dealing with a personality driven system. When no action taken by a person you support must ever be criticized, when we are encouraged to just trust an authority with no knowledge of their actions, when we are given the opportunity to vote for a person instead of actions, we are dealing with a personality driven system. This allows us no real control over our governance or the actions taken by our society at all. In representative democracy, far more of the public's time is spent debating what ought to be completely irrelevant personal attributes and studying politicians instead of policy.

A democratic ideal is a system of laws written to apply equally to all people in all cases. Many states have been attempting to circumvent those laws by reclassifying people as 'terrorists' or 'terrorist groups' and claiming that these groups are not allowed the same rights as others, in direct contradiction to the underlying principles. 'Two wrongs don't make a right', once a commonly repeated cliché, is now almost never heard. It is widely accepted that wrongs towards some people, in some cases, are a 'necessary evil'.

The new power of personality driven systems is being illustrated in wars where all effort is expended trying to cloud or identify who is behind each group of fighters, seen horribly in places like Syria and the Democratic Republic of Congo. The effort to identify groups is meant to aid allegiances and guide people in supporting one group of men with guns committing atrocities or another. An action or idea driven system would reject all who commit atrocities equally and support those building society. That is an incredibly simplistic statement when applied to the two cases above, but the root evil of investing in men with guns instead of people building societies is recognized in all areas of the world which suffer permanent 'instability'. The solution of just identifying 'the good guys' or deciding 'there are no good guys' was created and is continually promoted by those selling the weapons.

Where once soldiers were regular civilians who left their everyday lives to fight in defence of their societies, and were therefore worthy of the highest honour and gratitude, those civilians are now called 'terrorists', 'militants' and 'unprivileged combatants' and we are informed they have no right to fight in wars and are in fact war criminals for doing so. The people who deserve honour, we are told, are professional paid killers, willing to do anything they are told, not in defence of their society but in offense to any country they are paid to attack. Our laws have been twisted to grant impunity to those we once reviled as mercenaries and make war criminals of those we once celebrated as heroes.

The disease of personality driven systems extends to entire groups, where the same action taken by one is terrorism, by the other is self defence. Most extreme are those who feel killing babies is justified if Israel is killing them, or those that feel the United States 2012 NDAA's provision for indefinite detainment of US citizens is horrifying, the US Patriot Act's same power over everyone without US citizenship not worthy of notice. The faults of personality driven systems have been called by many names, racism, sexism, ageism, nationalism and more, but all of those - isms mean the same thing. People are being judged as nouns instead of verbs.

If instead of supporting nouns, we supported ideas and actions, it would be far easier to follow our chosen principles in all cases.

The ground breaking social theorists, Anonymous, have attempted in the past years to create a hierarchy of information, an oligarchy of ideas, in an attempt to escape the pitfalls of personality driven governance. Memes are a perfect example of concise ideas being shared for the value of their information with no need of further authority. Memes can also be used to circumvent censorship. Sina Weibo users talking about May 35th and other dates to mean the June 4, 1989 Tiannanmen Square anniversary is an example of ideas overcoming language control. China has the fastest moving memes of anywhere in the world due to the speed of their censors, and they have developed ingenuous idea and action driven systems to avoid retribution on personalities. The Sunday stroll of the short lived Jasmine Revolution [14] is one of many examples of gamified mass protests which everyone can play without direct instruction from an authority.

The promotion of ideas also allows ideas to be evaluated and fact checked on their own merits rather than accepted or rejected based on acceptance of the source. This is the best method of impartial evaluation since bad data can come from good places and vice versa. It is also the only way to be heard for voices which are marginalized otherwise. An idea based culture, where seeming majority opinions are rejected in favour of facts and individual assessment, is also the only real defence against astroturfers and persona management software, used online to simulate mass support where there is none.

Personality based systems have been fought for several years by citizen journalists who rejected the idea that only news from official channels was 'trustworthy' or 'safe' and have largely won that battle. There are still many battles ahead before people cease to be considered above reproach or failure and ideas are accepted for consideration blindly. In many ways, we are moving into more entrenched personality based systems with online celebrity influence wielding more power than ever, but it is also more obviously ridiculous now, and we have more power to revoke celebrity influence if we choose.

The first right of any person in an idea driven society must be the right to communicate. Without communication there is no way to safeguard our other rights or for us to participate fully in a society

When your right to communicate is interrupted by those who would be your voice, your face or your representative, you are being subjected to the governance of another. Horizontal governance does not mean no one gets a voice, it means everyone does. A person or group who attempts to suppress the voices of others is attempting to seize control. Official group channels are representative governance, regardless of consensus that may or may not lie behind them. A person who interprets another's voice instead of amplifying it is assuming control over the originator.

People giving a 'face' to a cause are standing between the people affected and the world. Media who pretend to write stories about groups whose voices are never heard but write almost universally through the lens of western men instead, are ensuring that all interpretations and solutions come from the same small segment of society. Wars are told from the point of view of arms dealers and politicians, disasters are interpreted by NGO's, most issues are never covered at all. Official channels decide what will or will not be revealed and media are rewarded for their obedience by access to more official information.

New media in its current form has made this worse instead of better. Journalists write about those powerful in social media to have their stories amplified by the same people. The news – celebrity symbiosis has escalated as writers vie for page views which can be granted by their chosen subject. We are at risk of having increasingly narrow news coverage as platforms like Twitter move to increase amplification of already powerful accounts and hide the less powerful opinions from view. As information and voice amplification become the new symbols of power, those who would assume control of society have moved to hoard voice amplification and control the message received by the public in new ways.

The pressure for marginalized groups to stay in their marginalized roles increases as does their opportunities to escape. While it was once possible to simply identify people in relation to a more powerful figure, as assistant, wife, staff, servant, serf, slave or other, the internet provided the opportunity for all to have an equal voice free of relation to others. The backlash to this freedom has been widespread even, or perhaps especially, in the groups fighting for social change.

Depending on the group, individual voices are told their message will receive greater amplification if it comes from another, the danger of speaking openly is so great they must be protected, their individual voices disrupt the harmony of consensus, or they are part of a collective and will be shunned if they dare speak with their own name. Assemblies ignore those who are too uncomfortable or unassertive to be heard in crowds and most are very unconcerned by the lack of input from these people as they 'had the opportunity' to speak. Differing levels of comfort or ability in this activity are rarely acknowledged. Assemblies and all other group and public activities have continued the oligarchies of the extroverts.

Most importantly, the free information beliefs of many groups which threaten power have been twisted to conflate credit theft with free information. Credit theft has absolutely nothing to do with free information. Copyright and patent laws which are structured to ensure fame and profit for those that can afford the fees and are the quickest to file forms have created a society and a history filled with people celebrated for creations they did not originate and filled also with creative people who died in poverty and anonymity because they did not have the gift of self promotion. While intellectual property rights need to be abolished, as they are inhibiting progress and being used as a tool of inappropriate permanent economic control and intimidation, idea credit rights need far more recognition and need to start being applied to the originator, not the copyright or patent holders.

Credit theft is a severe impediment to equality. It is as common now as ever for a person with access to powerful forums to pick up an idea from a person unable to reach the public and use it to enhance their own reputation. This is frequently brushed off in groups fighting for societal change as 'the hive' owns the idea, everyone does the role they choose, and it just so happens that the role most suitable to those in power (western men) is interviews, public speaking, books, etc., while the silent and unrecognized work is more suitable to the introverted or those without the power to take the stage. Any criticism or resentment is met with outrage that the originator cares more for their own fame than 'the cause'.

Credit for one's work or ideas is the right of every person. Credit provides the human dignity of societal recognition, approval and belonging. Credit for ideas and actions is an inherent part of personal identity. Unlike copying, which is not theft, taking credit deprives the rightful owner of it and is theft. There is no need to ever hide the origin of information unless the ultimate goal is to isolate them and suppress or twist their messages or use their work to glorify another.

A person who takes your idea and information to use and build upon is your collaborator, tester and colleague. A person who takes your credit or your voice is your enemy, a thief who steals your societal recognition and approval for themselves and would be your tyrant.

People grieve more and feel more importance is due to those they hear of more. Even on social media, the deaths of three people in a Boston marathon bombing[15] caused immediate international hysteria compared to the delayed response to the deaths of over a thousand in a factory collapse in Bangladesh[16] or the almost non-existent response to possibly two or three hundred civilians massacred by the Nigerian military[17] all within weeks of each other. A young western male doing anything that can be mislabelled as hacking can occupy international news for any reason or none. When he is also a journalist, the result is the exhaustive and entirely unwarranted international coverage of the firing of Reuters social media editor Matthew Keys or the equally irrational coverage of all things Anonymous and Lulzsec. Any story involving a girl with a sewing machine or a grandmother in Africa has no chance at all of being in the news. If it becomes necessary to cover those continually marginalized groups, they are presented within the lens of what western men think of them. The Rohingya genocide[18] and ritual murders in Gabon[19] were both ignored until Anonymous gave international media an angle they preferred, one profiling western male hackers.

To allow local governance and solutions, local voices must be the ones which formulate problems and create dialogue. People who are currently faceless and voiceless do not need another to be their face and voice.

Freedom of speech means equal voices for all and amplification where necessary, not the freedom of western men to drown out all other voices. We need a system where urgent local news can be collected and amplified globally when necessary, and where the people of the world decide which news is important, not official news channels or celebrity nodes.

Expertise without oligarchy

Chapter 13

While most action based systems can be completely open to participation by anyone, there are situations where an elite level of knowledge and accreditation of some sort is necessary prior to participation. Complicated surgery or engineering are examples of this type of work. While accreditation can and should come from the user group and be completely transparent and permeable, ability in many cases can only be reviewed by those who have attained an above average level of specialized knowledge. In these cases, there must be peer acknowledged levels of expertise attached to specific people, a situation not compatible with pure stigmergy or horizontal action.

Idea based systems such as some scientific research, which should be open to all contributions, require extensive feedback and peer review of ideas, both to identify signal from noise and to provide knowledge bridges between elite levels of knowledge and casual users. In many specialized systems such as the pharmaceutical industry, the entire user group has an urgent interest in ensuring that ideas are properly audited but few have the interest or ability to inform themselves to the level necessary to be able to audit. No one has the time to inform themselves to an expert level of knowledge in every system which affects them, even if that information is completely transparent and available to all. In these systems, ideas need to be promoted by those users qualified to understand them.

It is necessary to define a form of elitism, of ideas or people, that will take advantage of expertise but not remove control of a system from the end users. Ignoring elite knowledge in favour of a pretense at completely horizontal governance will not eliminate elitism, it will only create hidden oligarchies dominated by those without the expertise required, usually celebrity personalities.

An epistemic community can be people or ideas, depending on the situation. Idea based systems should promote ideas instead of people

In allowing this form of elitism, ultimate choice must always be left with the entire user group. An epistemic community is a knowledge resource only. Superior knowledge can only be forced to work for the wellbeing of the entire user group if authority remains with the entire user group and the epistemic community is forced to remain completely transparent and permeable. Science may dream of brilliant innovations, but the user group controls whether those are implemented or created. This authority also provides the incentive for transparency and knowledge bridges to explain reasoning to the entire group.

As in stigmergy, votes in a concentric group are frequently replaced by actions, as expert review will show the options most likely to bring the best results. This information is then available to all and those options will, barring outside factors, be accepted as best practices by most of the user group. The celebrated hive mind behind recent actions has never actually existed in practice. The hive takes actions, but ideas originate with individuals. On every occasion depicted as a mass hive action, there has been epistemic community or solitary planning initiating a butterfly effect. Even when these planning groups are theoretically open to all, they are in actuality only open to those with knowledge of them. Acknowledging epistemic communities does not create them, it simply brings them into the open and allows any member of the user group to participate.

An epistemic community can be people or ideas, depending on the situation. Idea based systems should promote ideas instead of people, a body of laws instead of a judiciary. Action in a specialized action based system can only be taken by those peer recognized as qualified, but meaningful input can come from a broad section of the user group and be evaluated and promoted by those qualified. Promoting ideas also allows auditing of an idea without all the unrelated distraction of attached personalities. There is an urgent need to separate expertise from popularity. Influence held by social media celebrities using strategies such as 'team followback', or influence peddling to earn social media rewards must not replace real trust networks of expertise recommendation. Nor must charisma and public relations skills replace knowledge in physical meetings.

In a concentric user group, people or ideas promoted to the center by their peer group receive greatest amplification and their findings will be audited, amplified and explained to the general public by outer circles. Concentric circles relate to sound amplification; the voices or ideas in the centre are amplified more greatly. They are not hierarchical as they have no direct control over the actions of anyone. While transparency will ensure that conversations at the centre are heard by all, it is unlikely that they will be understood by those with no knowledge of the system. It is not reasonable to expect those in the epistemic community to explain their reasoning to every member of the user group and attempt to educate every member to an elite level of understanding, but those of the user group with an interest have a right to education and understanding of that which effects them.

Communication should not be the full responsibility of the experts in the centre, but should be carried over expertise bridges by full transparency and user participation. It is the responsibility of each user in an open system to educate themselves to their own level of comfort using the data and user population at each level to inform themselves. Their input and decision making impact would then be commensurate with the expertise they acquire. The epistemic community in the centre should not need to protect themselves from demands or attacks from completely uninformed users. The circles of expertise which promoted them to the centre should also verify and explain their findings to the outer circles.

Ideas can never be furthered if discussion is always at the level of the novice, and the ideas of an expert can only be tested by other experts with equal understanding of the topic. In a concentric user group, the receptive field is stronger near the centre, so informed opinions will be heard more clearly by experts in the centre, but full transparency will allow anyone from any part of the system to be as informed as they wish to be by any other part.

Knowledge bridges allow discussion to be held at every level of expertise and corrected by those with greater knowledge. Knowledge bridges also allow input from casual users to be instantly promoted to be heard by the epistemic community, if the user group finds the points valid. Knowledge bridges need to ensure that the best ideas are promoted and disseminated, regardless of the attractiveness or popularity of the person with the expertise.

Acceptance of ideas must be controlled by the entire user group, and the user group must always have the power to shun, thereby removing power from, any peer promoted expert. This is necessary to avoid a closed oligarchy, but it must be approached warily so that the amplified voices in the center are the true experts, not the most populist and attractive choices. It is incumbent on the user group to protect the center from celebrity grabbing manipulation if they are not to recreate the populist systems of representative democracy.

In representative democracy, we have learned that people, in general, prefer to place their faith in leaders who are like them instead of leaders who are so expert they do not understand them. In order to avail ourselves of the greatest expertise on each topic, we must place our most knowledgeable experts in a position of transparent authority while also providing a knowledge bridge leading from their ideas to the casually interested observer. According to Leta Hollingworth's research, to be a leader of their contemporaries a child must be more intelligent but not too much more intelligent than them. A discrepancy of more than about 30 points of IQ does not allow for leadership, or even respect or effective communication. The same principle appears to hold for levels of knowledge on a given topic.

Hollingworth notes: *A lesson which many gifted persons never learn as long as they live is that human beings in general are inherently very different from themselves in thought, in action, in general intention, and in interests. Many a reformer has died at the hands of a mob which he was trying to improve in the belief that other human beings can and should enjoy what he enjoys. This is one of the most painful and difficult lessons that each gifted child must learn, if personal development is to proceed successfully. It is more necessary that this be learned than that any school subject be mastered. Failure to learn how to tolerate in a reasonable fashion the foolishness of others leads to bitterness, disillusionment, and misanthropy.* [20]

This loss of expertise is a tragedy for both the experts and society. There needs to be a method of organization that will use all expertise at the level it will be most effective and avoid communication barriers. Those with elite knowledge need to be able to have relatively quiet conversations with others that can expand and audit the knowledge base while still providing complete transparency, permeability and control for the rest of the user group.

Most manifestations of attempts at horizontal governance attempt to deny all elitism by discouraging or forbidding it in any form and denying its necessity. Whether or not oligarchy exists, elitism most certainly does, in every field that requires expertise beyond that of a novice. To not allow elitism would be to not allow expertise, which would cripple any society. Elite levels of knowledge exist today for many reasons, exclusion of the majority of the population from education and access being the biggest. As an ideal in an open transparent society, anyone would be capable of attempting to contribute to elite knowledge resources, but limitations of interest or ability will still exclude all but a few. This is not an evil if it is properly controlled, and it is in fact the best way to ensure decisions based on real expertise instead of connections and other sources of power.

Where elite knowledge exists, there will always be elite conversations. If there are not clubs which require membership, then there are parties such as that which started Martha Stewart's troubles, or just conversations that are held above the level of a novice's understanding. The keys to allowing elite expertise but not allowing for elite conspiracies are transparency and knowledge bridges. If Martha had instantly tweeted the conversation at her elite party and people had rapidly spread its meaning to a novice level, there would have been no unfair advantage in her conversation.

Oligarchies appear to be inevitable for many reasons. The reasons related to control of the work of others for achieving goals we can overcome by using stigmergy, consensus and other tools, but there is a place in society for an elite system of knowledge, and that knowledge will always be a source of power. The key to preventing elite knowledge from becoming a tyrannical oligarchy is to maintain control by the user group over action and decisions and treat epistemic communities always as a knowledge resource, not a governing power. Shunning can be used to instantly remove power in an open system, keeping the real power within the user group, not the epistemic community. No system of elite knowledge must ever become unassailable. When combined with stigmergy, the work produced in systems with transparent, permeable epistemic communities may finally be of the highest standard we can attain and the work environments will allow autonomous control for all.

Once, there were exclusive clubs and organizations where people could go to isolate themselves and rule the world in elite company. They need to be replaced with transparent, helpful epistemic communities which are part of the community. The Communist Party of China, the Vatican and the Davos group are all examples of oligarchies which no longer have any legitimate reason to conduct their activities in secrecy and with no input from their user groups.

If power from property ownership and hierarchical organizations are removed, knowledge and celebrity will be the dominant sources of power and the places to watch for a new oligarchy.

Chapter 14

Shunning, trolling and photoshopping

In concentric circles, experts are peer promoted based on reputation instead of certification by an external authority. Each user of a system can review the work of the active members, both directly and through the expert review of the active member's peers, instead of placing their faith in a third party certification. Additionally, experts can be created by the system itself as users develop knowledge, expertise and reputation and move towards the centre. Third party authorities such as universities are no longer necessary. It is essential that peer review of expertise is done fairly and without personality based bias.

In an inclusive society, shunning is the most effective punishment for violation of the social contract. Shunning removes the offending person from some or all of the benefits of belonging to a society. As the prison systems can attest, particularly those that practice the torture of solitary confinement, the effects of shunning are terrible to humans, an inherently highly social species.

In an otherwise non-coercive society, shunning is also the most effective way of removing power from a member of an epistemic community. Ideas which no one follows will wither and die, as they only become powerful with the agreement of the actors. Conversations which engage no one will fall silent. Shunning is a very powerful tool and should be recognized as such, and not used lightly or maliciously to block access to power.

In a permeable system open to input by all, trolling is used to assess expertise where it is not immediately apparent and allow or block participation in conversations of elite knowledge. The jargon employed in most specialized fields is used to facilitate this trolling, as well as inside jokes, conversations that allow quick assessment of knowledge levels and traps to make the less knowledgeable participant appear foolish. Trolling frequently becomes ad hominem attack to

> **Shunning is a very powerful tool and should be recognized as such, and not used lightly or maliciously to block access to power.**

drive a participant from a conversation if they have been found to not have the appropriate level of knowledge. While the first form is an expedient way to keep conversations at an elite level and allow input only from those qualified, as well as to exclude sock puppets and astroturfing online, trolling is a form of shunning and should never be used to drive away people who are qualified or those who are honestly trying to learn.

Actions which would be celebrated from western men frequently become discredited and downplayed if it is found they originated from a marginalized group. In *We Are Anonymous*[21], a work celebrating western male 'hackers', the resentment of the female author at the necessary inclusion of a few women in the story is palpable. Of Laurelai we are told *"she was also spending about twelve hours a day online while her mother looked after her two kids."* Of Jennifer Emick, who correctly discovered the real life identity of Lulzsec member Sabu, she *"often got the kids to cook dinner. They ate a lot of pizza."* Emick was married, with teenagers. Not once is the reader told what the two far younger little girls in Sabu's sole custody were eating while he was online. Every woman who accomplishes anything newsworthy has her personal life examined for neglect of other aspects so it can be a story of failure instead of one of success. *"Rumour had it that No had gained her status by flirting with other male operators."* The male operators who gained their status by either flirting with or befriending other men do not have their accomplishment discredited.

Frequently, trolling and shunning are used to keep some from positions of power. Sexual and other harassment to prevent people from speaking, meetings conducted in places or in a manner to make them uncomfortable for some, or harsher standards and far more trolling of those who are automatically assumed to be inferior are examples of oligarchies defending their turf. Current epistemic communities are the new private clubs. The same standards of admittance should be applied to all. Internet anonymity for many was akin to emerging from Plato's cave with the ability, for the first time, to join all conversations and be treated as an equal as long as the anonymity was unbroken. That ability needs to be defended for all, even in a system where people are known.

Photoshopping is another way of ensuring that credit is given to only a few. Almost all actions and bodies of knowledge involve several people. It is simple to exclude some as being peripheral and highlight others as central without much notice being taken. Rosalind Franklin's work could be called peripheral to Watson and Crick's, perhaps not as important, and the choice of the two over the one downplayed. But when you begin to see everyone but western men drastically underrepresented in every list of important people, it raises the possibility that perhaps everyone else is being photoshopped out of the stories with inferior titles, inferior media attention and inferior idea crediting.

Women historically come with built in anonymity; everything they say has been proxy routed through the nearest man and given no credence until it was. The work of introverts is claimed by extroverts and the work of voices discredited is claimed by accepted personalities. Blogs reference each other as the corporate media refuses to name them. Western men own media empires which hire western men who interview western men. The misogynist-labelled Reddit ensures those articles featuring men are widely read[22] [23]. Wikipedia's over 95% male editors have been accused constantly of a gender bias in editing[24], as well as being an amplification and glorification of western male dominated corporate media. Wikipedia's reliance on corporate sources ensures corporate control over knowledge. They produce a reference populated largely with western men in positions of influence which is used to determine online measures of influence. Influence ranking sites fall victim to the Hawthorne Effect and instead of documenting influence they create it. All of this data is used to determine who sits on panels and boards, who is given awards, who is hired for positions of influence and the image we all carry in our heads of what an expert looks like.

Women especially, are defined in relation to men, as assistant, secretary, aide, etc. In this way, they can perform the same or more work, but credit for their work and ideas is preemptively assigned to the person they are defined in relation to and they are locked out of receiving influence. Non western voices are put into sub-categories. They are not 'thought leaders', they are 'African thought leaders'. Like 'women's issues', these sub-categories become ghettos where no one ever looks except for tokenism. Those refused recognition leave in frustration, as they must produce many times the content to receive any recognition and must not complain or they will be further marginalized. Young students are left with no mentors in a system where those similar to them are erased.

The exclusion is so pervasive the US media even overwhelmingly go to men for opinions on 'women's issues' as seen in the following chart. For general issues such as politics, the conversation has revolved around men with guns and money for so long, with the rare article on victimized women, it is as if no one even realizes there are alternative stories, such as all the people building society instead of destroying it. The token women in media are not taken seriously as mainstream news sources unless they only report on men and interview men. Without these alternative stories, people are left with the choice of supporting one group of men with guns and money or another, choosing one as 'good guys' and the other as 'bad guys', despite the similarity of actions. The story of creators is considered not as newsworthy as the story of destroyers. Killing people is both newsworthy and a respected career while giving birth is neither. These limited views dictate the structure of our society.

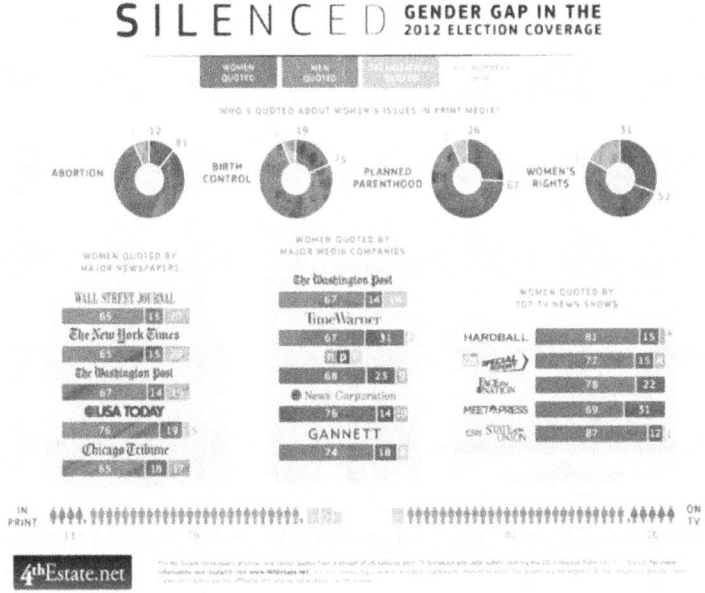

Figure 3: Women's voices in media

In many or most cases, this exclusion is not deliberate. Those doing the excluding are not even aware they are doing it. When you are standing in the spotlight, you can't see the shadows. Many times it seems those in the spotlight are unaware of the existence of others on the stage. It is essential to maintain transparent, idea and action driven systems with vigilant user groups to keep epistemic communities inclusive and open.

Chapter 15

Epistemic communities in action based systems

In open source software, the code for each project is available for all to see. Even if the end user cannot understand the code, they can go to discussion groups and read or listen to programmers who have read and audited the code, hear their discussions, and watch them find bugs and discuss alternative solutions. The people with the greater knowledge of the system will provide knowledge bridges for people at a more novice level. Good ideas from these discussions can be read, discussed and possibly implemented by the developers as well. Open source software with forums open to all are a perfect working example of fully transparent and audited systems of elite knowledge. While the decisions are made by the developers, review and acceptance or rejection of the software is the right of the user group. If the developers refuse to listen to the user group and another development team is willing to work on the project, the original code can be forked and modified to meet the user requirements.

Traditional systems primarily use a supposedly representative sample of the user group to provide periodic feedback. This feedback is delivered as percentages of the population which ignores the importance of the individual. From an individual perspective, the chance of dying of a side effect from a pharmaceutical is either 0% or 100%. Group statistics have no effect on individual experience. Transparent user groups allow feedback and ideas from the entire user group, an automatic testing and validation system in place continually throughout development and operation. Risks which are 'statistically insignificant' become extremely important when they happen to an active participant in the user group community. This more accurately reflects a real society vs a system of dissociation.

The github model of open software, with replaceable lords of a fiefdom, may be improved on in a system where the entire epistemic community operates by consensus, but as long as there is transparency and the ability for anyone to fork the code and start anew, oligarchies can still be avoided. Online courses such as those offered by Coursera where students teach each other and have direction from an epistemic community of instructors with knowledge bridges of graduates and fellow students is another example of a concentric circle in the cases where the course material is released as creative commons. CryptoParties are another.

Chapter 16

Celebrity and thought leaders

As we ponder how to create action and idea based systems, the internet, and so the world, is becoming more personality based than ever before in history. The internet is rapidly transforming from being page centric to people centric. The hive mind has become me the people. As liquid democracy type representation becomes more accepted, personal branding for power becomes even more entrenched. Anonymity and group work are being pushed aside in favour of personal celebrity for all.

Along with celebrity have come tools to measure celebrity. The first such tool was Wikipedia, a glorification and amplification of corporate media and English speakers with technical skills. Now Klout and similar platforms are taking influence measurement further and not just creating celebrity oligarchies but also dictating the terms of engagement between the oligarchies and the user group with their algorithms. These tools do not just measure influence, they create it, and unchecked, their algorithms will dictate the terms of our new society. If Klout scores people higher for engagement, celebrity thought leaders will engage. If Klout scores higher for engaging with higher ranked celebrities, the powerful will become more powerful and even unassailable. If Klout celebrities score higher for only interacting with and following each other, we will have a closed oligarchy.

Klout is one example, but there are many powerful online tools doing the same. The Google search controversy, over whether Google should show people what they already like instead of presenting a more realistic, broader view is another. Even a search engine presenting the most commonly sought result instead of a random selection helps entrench already entrenched ideas. Sponsored 'who to follow' groups, or Twitter's event pages with only certain tweeters shown, ensure more power for the powerful. A short time ago, if you wished for real influence, as opposed to influence created to sell to marketers, cheating by gaming the influence measurement systems wouldn't help, because the tricks brought no real influence.

Now real influence follows the appearance of influence. In addition to gaming scams, it is openly possible to buy influence, for instance by paying Facebook to promote your page or Twitter to promote a tweet. While Twitter was a data driven breakthrough for online society, where no one needed acceptance to begin interacting, this is becoming less true all the time. Anyone can speak, but voices are amplified as favours given and received and the rules change as accounts grow more powerful. Pure data driven systems are, unfortunately, nearly impossible in a world of spam and astroturfing software. With the vast amounts of data in our world, celebrity amplification of good ideas is needed. The first reaction to this realization by those wishing for a horizontal community was to create group hubs, but these have largely and correctly been felled by the problems with group affiliation.

An idea popularized by celebrity personality endorsement without knowledgeable input can subsequently be exposed as simplistic, factually incorrect or otherwise flawed by those with deeper knowledge, but the celebrity endorsement can drown the expert knowledge. The Kony 2012 campaign was a striking example of celebrity endorsement drowning local knowledge[25].

Celebrity endorsement can drown the expert knowledge.

The influence of celebrities from entertainment and sports industries over unrelated topics is illogical but widespread, and they are more than ever expected to use that influence in areas completely outside their knowledge sphere. When actors Yao Chen and Chen Kui Kun posted support against censorship to Southern Weekend newspaper on Sina Weibo, it appeared more newsworthy than a statement from the United Nations would be.

Even within the entertainment industry, which may be thought to be within the sphere of celebrity expertise, most had hoped for grass roots driven promotion to replace corporate promotion. Instead, we find corporate sponsorship replaced by a tweet from Justin Bieber, which launched stars such as Carly Rae Jepsen and Psy far more immediately and effectively than a label ever dreamed of doing.

All of the above sounds very discouraging, but it really isn't. The first step in any cleaning and organizing is to drag everything out to the open to be sorted and that is what has happened with celebrity. None of this influence is new. It is in fact a far more toned down, accessible and transparent version of the celebrity and influence peddling we have had for years. It is palatable for an individual you choose whether or not to follow to recommend an artist that you can choose to watch or not without diluting your supply of alternative choices. Compared to the control once exerted by music labels, this does not seem evil. Paper citations in academia or votes in Hollywood's Academy Awards are no less subject to influence peddling.

Much of the undue influence is inherently repulsive to most people, and they have already begun to combat it. The Kony 2012 campaign suffered an immediate, if largely unheard, backlash from the people actually in the region. Today, those rebuttals would be even more immediate and well amplified. Even the traditional pundits from old corporate media hardly dare write any more about regions they are not resident of. Soon, all such foreign punditry will be replaced by local voices and news will be reported by those it is happening to as audiences will demand that level of informed opinion.

A cultural shift is required around celebrity. Celebrity was created to distract attention from issues the true oligarchies did not want scrutinized. The public's 'right to know' was transferred from the business of the government to the plastic surgery of an entertainer. This type of celebrity is no longer needed and it is becoming rapidly diluted as the general population occupy celebrity by being Tumblr famous, Twitter famous, etc. Expertise is already largely separate from celebrity. Voice amplification will soon be merely a job and a fairly boring one at that.

Until this cultural shift is complete, it is dangerous to concentrate even knowledge based celebrity in one individual or group of individuals, and there must be continuous intelligent auditing by the user groups. Open epistemic communities generally are plagued with members, who may or may not be qualified to be there, but they play the outer circles against the inner and create a human interest story of themselves. Their fame and popular support makes them impossible to challenge or shun. This is distracting and detracts from the work of the community. User groups must ensure that while they watch their communities for inclusiveness, they do not allow themselves to be manipulated this way.

The tools to moderate a celebrity or expertise oligarchy are now in the hands of the people. Hopefully, the user groups will moderate, exercise their ability to shun for bad behaviour and refuse to allow control to leave the entire user group. There is no reason why a person with a learning disability should be less happy or satisfied than one with a brilliant mind, or why gardening should not be as rewarding a life work choice as participating in an epistemic community or acquiring internet celebrity. It is an artificially controlled environment of privilege that makes one seem better than the other. This is easily overcome in a population not controlled by their financial system.

Heather Marsh

Heather Marsh

Stigmergy

Chapter 17

Stigmergy is a mechanism of indirect coordination between agents or actions. The principle is that the trace left in the environment by an action stimulates the performance of a next action, by the same or a different agent. In that way, subsequent actions tend to reinforce and build on each other, leading to the spontaneous emergence of coherent, apparently systematic activity. Stigmergy is a form of self organization. It produces complex, seemingly intelligent structures, without need for any planning, control, or even direct communication between the agents. – Wikipedia

C ertain ideas are powerful enough to create a butterfly effect, a swarm that will not be stopped by any restraining force. The civil rights movement in the United States was one such idea which no amount of opposition could prevent. The power of stigmergy was proven in that and many other points in history. Stigmergy is the action based twin of an idea based system. If there are no official authorities, anyone can act to further an idea and it is up to the society or user group to accept or reject the act.

A personality based system can never allow for mass collaboration on a global scale without representation such as that seen in organizations like the United Nations. If the world is to move away from representation and allow all voices to be heard, we need to find methods of collaboration which work with idea and action based systems. Concentric user groups with epistemic communities and knowledge bridges may work for idea based systems. For action, stigmergy seems the best option. Currently, the typical response to a situation which requires an action is to create a noun, in the form of a committee, commission, organization, corporation, NGO, government body, etc. Far too often, the action never appears at all as the focus is always on the organization and the personalities involved instead.

Most systems are now run by competitive organizations. Competition creates redundancy, is slow and wastes resources on idea protection, advertisement, and more. Competition also requires secrecy which blocks progress and auditing and causes lost opportunities and ideas. Patents and copyrights further limit speed and the potential for mass input of ideas. Collaboration between the people with the greatest expertise does not happen unless they are hired by the same project.

The alternative to competition has traditionally been cooperation. This is most effective only in groups of two to eight people. For groups larger than 25, cooperation is agonizingly slow, an exercise in personality management which quickly degenerates into endless discussion and soothing of ruffled feathers. It is extremely vulnerable to agent provocateurs and, in large scale groups, very seldom accomplishes anything of value. Cooperation traditionally operates on the democratic principle that all voices are equal, so it does not allow for leaders, or users with greater expertise, energy or understanding to have greater influence than those on the periphery. Cooperation wastes a great deal of time and resources in both discussing and discussing the discussions. In an action based system, this discussion is rarely required as the opinion of those not doing the work is probably of little value unless it is solicited advice from a trusted knowledgeable party.

Cooperation and consensus based systems are usually dominated by extroverted personalities who make decisions to control the work of others and are justly resented by those doing the actual work. Most workers do not enjoy the hierarchical systems shown in the chart below, as they lose autonomy, mastery and creative control over their own work. The feeling at the bottom is no different whether there is a horizontal or a hierarchical structure making the decisions. Cooperative systems frequently use consensus or votes to make decisions for the entire group. These methods may not produce the best results as many people may not understand the work if they are not actually doing it, and they may demand things they would never be willing to do themselves. Consensus based systems are also prone to the 'hive mind' appropriation of credit for individual ideas and labour which causes further resentment.

Figure 4: Hierarchical system

Figure 5: Consensus hierarchy

In the Stigmergy picture below, all workers have full autonomy to create as they wish. The power of the user group is in the ability to accept or reject the work. Since there is no officially designated person to perform a task, the users are free to create alternatives if they do not like what they are offered. Workers are free to create regardless of acceptance or rejection. In the picture below, some work may be accepted by the largest group, some alternatives for a different user group, some only by a small group, and sometimes the worker will be alone with their vision.

Figure 6: Stigmergy

In all cases, the worker is still free to create as they wish. History has shown no drastically innovative ideas that received instant mainstream acceptance and history also shows that radically new ideas are most often the result of solitary vision. To leave control of work to group consensus only is to cripple innovation.

Chapter 18

Stigmergic Collaboration

In a competitive environment, a new idea is jealously guarded, legally protected and shrouded in secrecy. Great effort is expended in finding supporters for the idea while also ensuring that it remains covered by legal protections such as non-disclosure agreements. The idea remains inextricably bound to the creator until it is legally transferred to another owner. All contributors work for the owner, not the idea. Contributors must then be rewarded by the owner which further limits the potential for development and wastes more resources in legal agreements, lawsuits, etc. Contributors have no interest in whether the project succeeds or fails and no motivation to contribute more than they are rewarded for.

If the idea is instead developed cooperatively, it must first be pitched by the originator, who will attempt to persuade a group to adopt the idea. The group must be in agreement with the idea itself and with every stage of its development. The majority of energy and resources are spent on communication, persuasion, and personality management, and the working environment is fraught with arguments and power struggles. Because the project is driven by a group, albeit a cooperative one, the group is still competitive with other similar outside projects, and still wastes resources and energy on secrecy, competitive evangelizing, etc. Both competitive and cooperative projects will die if the group that runs the project leaves and both will attract or repel contributors based on the personalities of the existing group. Both are hierarchical systems where individuals need to seek permission to contribute. Both focus on the authority of personalities to approve a decision instead of focusing on the idea or action itself.

Stigmergy is neither competitive nor cooperative. With stigmergy, an initial idea is freely given, and the project is driven by the idea, not by a personality or group of personalities. No individual needs permission (competitive) or consensus (cooperative) to propose an idea or initiate a project. There is no need to discuss or vote on the idea. If an idea is exciting or necessary it will attract interest. The interest attracted will be from people actively involved in the system and willing to put effort into carrying the project further, not empty votes from people with little interest or involvement. Since the project is supported or rejected based on contributed effort, not empty votes, input from people with more commitment to the idea will have greater weight. Stigmergy also puts individuals in control over their own work. They do not need group permission to tell them what system to work on or what part to contribute.

The person with the initial idea may or may not carry the task further. Evangelizing the idea is voluntary, by a group that is excited by the idea. They may or may not be the ones to carry it out. It is unnecessary to seek start up funding and supporters. If an idea is good it will receive the support required. (In practice, that is not true yet, as few people have the free time to put into volunteer projects because most are tied to compulsory work under the existing financial system. Additionally, we still live in a personality driven system where only powerful personalities are heard.) Secrecy and competition are unnecessary because once an idea is given, it and all new development belongs to anyone who chooses to work on it. Anyone can

> **All ideas are accepted or rejected based on the needs of the system. Responsibility and rights for the system rest with the entire user group, not just the creators.**

submit work for approval; the idea cannot die or be put on hold by personalities. Acceptance or rejection is for the work contributed, not the person contributing it. All ideas are accepted or rejected based on the needs of the system. Responsibility and rights for the system rest with the entire user group, not just the creators. There is no need for people to leave the system based on personality conflicts as there is no need for communication outside of task completion, and there are usually plenty of jobs with complete autonomy. As no one owns the system, there is no need for a competing group to be started to change ownership.

Stigmergy provides little scope for agent provocateurs as only the needs of the system are considered. Anyone working against the system's functionality is much easier to see and prevent than someone blocking progress with endless discussion and creation of personality conflicts. Because the system is owned by all, there is also no one leader to target.

Movements driven by stigmergy usually fluctuate between periods of stagnation where most are willing to tolerate the current state and upheavals where a weakness once named becomes unbearable by all and is changed by another mass movement. The civil rights movement in the United States was itself a continuation of the anti slavery movement. Once the feeling of injustice past the point of tolerance spread, stigmergy ensured the idea would not be suppressed. While neither the upheaval to abolish slavery nor the upheaval for the civil rights movement have succeeded in providing racial equality in the US, both made radical progress and the idea will continue until equality is achieved.

Chapter 19

Splintering nodes

As work progresses and core team and members grow, more interested and dedicated personalities emerge which begin to steer direction. Specialties are formed around the core team's interests as the core team produces the most work and the work most valued by the rest of the user group. Systems beyond a certain level of complexity begin to lack coherence as the group's energy and focus moves from broad to narrow, following the interests of the core team and the availability of resources. Parts of the original system may be left undone.

As more members are added, more will experience frustration at limited usefulness or autonomy. Some of these members will have an interest in the work left undone and they will create a new node of like minded members and new people to take care of the undone work. Alternatively, casual users and observers of the system, who lack the desire or expertise to be a more active part of the original system, will see a different need created and start a new node. Rather than the traditional corporate model of endless acquisition and expansion, stigmergy encourages splintering into different nodes. Because each individual is responsible only for their own work, and no one can direct a group of workers, expansion means more work for the individual, a self limiting prospect. As a system grows, the additional work requires either additional resources or splintering. As communication is easier and there is more autonomy in smaller groups, splintering is the more likely outcome of growth.

Communication between nodes of a system is on an as needed basis. Transparency allows information to travel freely between the various nodes, but a formal relationship or communication method is neither necessary nor desirable. Information sharing is driven by the information, not personal relationships. If data is relevant to several nodes it will be immediately transmitted to all. No formal meetings between official personalities are necessary.

Any node can disappear without affecting the network, and the remaining necessary functionality of that node can be taken up by others. Nodes which find they are performing the same tasks will likely join, or one will be rendered obsolete by lack of use. New nodes are only created to fulfill a new need or provide greater functionality. It is inefficient to have the same task performed twice, and that only occurs if a second group discovers an alternative method that the first group is unwilling to adopt. In that case, the best system will win the most support from the user group, the other will die or remain as a valued alternative. Any user can contribute to the node which best matches their interests and abilities, or contribute to multiple nodes.

A new system of governance or collaboration that does not follow a competitive hierarchical model will need to employ stigmergy in most of its action based systems. It is neither reasonable nor desirable for individual thought and action to be subjugated to group consensus in matters which do not affect the group and it is frankly impossible to accomplish complex tasks if every decision must be presented for approval. That is the biggest weakness of the hierarchical model. The incredible success of so many internet projects are the result of stigmergy, not cooperation, and it is stigmergy that will help us build quickly, efficiently and produce results far better than any of us can foresee at the outset.

A world without a

financial system

Chapter 20

A n overriding concern of many people participating in protests in recent years has been the financial system. From the September 17, 2011 protests against financial institutions and the symbolism of Occupy Wall Street to the widespread discussion of alternative currencies, money received more air time than even human rights and war. The current human rights atrocities and endless wars did not even cause the Arab Spring. It was the unfairness of the economic systems (starting with the fining of a fruit seller in Tunisia) which was the initial driving force behind the 2011 protests. The current speculation regarding the possible collapse of the financial system focuses on possible replacements.

With all of this attention, it would be easy to assume that financial systems must be a very important part of any future economy. But must they? Before we discuss alternative systems or how to repair our current system, we need to look at why we need a financial system at all. If we define the function of our financial systems, form should follow easily, be it community currency, barter, p2p digital, resource based or other.

Heather Marsh

Chapter 21

Dissociation

The current financial system functions as a means to tie the work that is done for corporations to basic essentials such as food and housing in an entirely artificial relationship. Despite an abundance of basic essentials, individuals or entire countries can be deprived of them based on the labour or rights they are providing to corporations. A system where banks, governments, and many other valueless institutions also stand between individuals and basic needs and demand payment completes the creation of true wage slavery where no worker can survive outside the system. By providing a complete disconnect between work required to produce basic essentials and ownership or access to them, this system also assures gross overabundance of resources for people who do no work of value at all. The financial system enables very inequitable distribution of resources.

155

Wages are commonly described as a motivator to work. We are told that no one would work if they were not paid. This is belied by the amount of people raising their children, cleaning their homes, tending their gardens, volunteering for fire departments and writing open source software and it is belied by cultures in myriad times and places which survived happily without a financial system. Women in all cultures are expected to do very difficult, time consuming, laborious and high risk unpaid work to give birth and raise children, and in many cultures they remain as an almost entirely unpaid foundation of slave labour that the rest of the economy is built upon. What is referred to as women's right to work is really the right to do paid corporate work. All of the work that benefits society is, has been or could easily be unpaid, while pay is only required for work that is harmful to society. Valuation of work rests with corporations and governments which ensure that workers will engage in pointlessly dangerous and immoral work that they would never do otherwise. People are paid to kill people. People are not paid to give birth. Is it now more socially acceptable to kill people than to give birth to people? Or is it just more immediately valuable to corporations?

Wages were created, not to motivate us to work, but to control our work. The jobs that corporations and governments have chosen to value are almost entirely busywork, pointless jobs that would not exist in another system, jobs including, but not limited to, everything in sales, finance, management, politics, and more. The end result of corporate work is far too much product and products and services that are detrimental to society and the environment. Any attempts to stop corporate work are met with the cry that to do so would cause job loss, which is promoted as a great evil as, under this system, jobs equal basic essentials. Jobs are always touted as being in short supply, valuable, and difficult to obtain, especially the 'good' jobs that pay the most money. Jobs are, of course, not remotely scarce. Any child can find hundreds of valuable things to do at any time, but these valuable jobs have not had an artificial monetary value associated with them.

Any for profit system is not going to have social or environmental goals as its mandate (even if it says it does) and a wage paying system is a for profit system. If profit were removed, all decisions would be made for social goals. Prison systems would be trying to rehabilitate prisoners or study to find why they were in violation of the law instead of just warehousing as many as possible, medical research would be trying to improve health instead of selling pharmaceuticals, and agriculture would be devoted to producing the most nutritious food in the most environmentally responsible way. Removing profit would also remove a great deal of the reason for competitiveness, secrecy and spying within organizations, along with a great deal of the redundancy of competing companies providing identical goods and services. Removing wages attached to a specific system would give every individual the freedom to leave any system they did not agree with or that began to malfunction due to core team problems, a better alternative system or other reason. Removing profit eradicates the need for ownership of knowledge and many other assets.

On an international level, the financial system serves to artificially control which countries are wealthy and which are not. Many of the most resource rich countries in the world have destitute populations and the multinational corporations that own the 'rights' to their resources remove the wealth to other countries. At a national level, the financial system allows banks, who have no need of housing, to hoard millions of houses while the children that used to live in them sleep in the streets. At an individual level, the equating of life's essentials with the financial system can control life or death, fulfillment or wasted potential, contentment or misery.

All of society's problems which could be solved by money were caused by money

Chapter 22

Social impact

P aid work creates poverty. Anyone not enabling the corporations and doing their work lives in fear of the legal and societal persecution that comes with poverty. Poverty is the hardest work of any available today. It is a very expensive lifestyle, entailing endless fines, charges and fees levied by the corporate and government world. It leaves no time to achieve any fulfillment, is a life threatening health risk, and is extremely damaging to all personal relationships. It is naturally almost universally dreaded.

Poverty is also regarded as a moral failure, as society needs to blame the victim to avoid blaming themselves for the situation the poor find themselves in. In this way, courage, duty, industry, thrift, kindness, loyalty – all of the traditional virtues may be replaced simply by wealth, the ultimate virtue respected in society today. The very word 'unemployed' states idleness, although anyone who has been poor knows how much work is involved. Wealth is used synonymously with success and achievement. Paid work artificially values one job above another (and subsequently the person doing that job above the other) regardless of individual preference. While manual work might be considered more enjoyable than executive work by most people, since it provides exercise, social interaction and purpose, the assigned values teach us to value pointless executive work instead.

Paid work occupies all of our time, and when we are outside the financial system poverty is a full time job. This acts to cripple all volunteer work such as community gardens and open source projects that would otherwise be done for free and may undermine the system of wage control over individuals.

Paid work creates poverty.

For those that volunteer anyway, the financial system ensures that their work, such as child rearing or innovative thought, is kept from ever resulting in any kind of independence and encourages those volunteers to collaborate with the corporate system to obtain security. Volunteer work is also subject to the same moral scrutiny as poverty, especially in recent years when a requirement of being poor is frequently the oxymoronic compulsory volunteer work associated with receiving basic essentials. Previously the domain of the rich and idle, therefore commendable, volunteer work has now become tainted with the stench of poverty, further limiting willing participants.

Paid work feeds a consumer economy, both by providing the means to purchase and creating the demand and need for products. If people had time to play, exercise and eat healthy food, they would need less medical care. If they had time to care for each other, they would not need institutions and NGO's for care. If they had time to help themselves and each other they would not require a vast array of sold products and services. They could also participate in a far wider variety of activities if they were not funneled into filling one role only.

The current financial system is necessary to control our work, to control our time, to create poverty, to create division and to force people to do work which is harmful to society.

Chapter 23

A modified system

It is possible, and frequently proposed, that the current financial system be modified to make it accessible for all to earn the basic essentials of life more easily. This could be done by having far more types of work valued, by providing various forms of charity, by forcing corporations to follow certain workplace standards and many other tweaks and regulations. All are, in the end, just modifications to the master slave relationship and none recognize the underlying flaws in the system. Who would be the authority valuing the work, administering the charity and enforcing the standards? Who has control of the wages? Whoever maintains authority over the work of others maintains the hierarchical system and prevents workers from having autonomy, mastery and control over their own work. This infantilization of workers, even in a system with worker's rights, limits innovation, decreases satisfaction, and prevents workers from reaching their full potential.

If there is any financial system, there will be coercion outside the benefit of society. If there is demand for a house and someone is paid to build a house, that person will be elevated above someone helping the ill or gardening. Building houses will then be seen as a more attractive choice of work, regardless of personal affinity or the needs of society. Where people are paid to build houses, houses will be destroyed instead of preserved, people will be convinced they need newer, bigger houses, and all of the trappings of capitalism will continue.

Chapter 24

A currency free system

I

t is possible for a society to function well with no financial system at all. Where surplus exists, it can be given, traded or pooled communally to ensure there is no want of basic essentials. The argument that only primitive societies can operate in such a fashion, our society is too complex, is not backed by any insurmountable obstacles. A moneyless system is unlikely to appear soon in its pure form, but it could exist to cover at least basic essentials or an expiring currency could be distributed as a guaranteed periodic income which would cover basic essentials. These options would a least ensure a society does not condemn a child to starvation because a parent cannot provide for them and it would relieve the pressing need to obey corporate authority. It would allow people to follow the path that for them provides the greatest satisfaction without being held to corporate slavery while we create an alternative system.

A great fear associated with abolishing wages or providing anything 'for free' is that some people may not work. This fear completely disregards the fact that there have always been people who will not work under the current system and they include the people receiving the highest monetary rewards. Nobody worries about those who are rich not working, just the poor. This seems to indicate a fear of shifting social status, not a fear of people not working. Because of the artificial monetary value assigned to some jobs, people who elect to do demanding and valuable work with no associated corporate wage are sneered at as 'welfare mothers', etc. and made to believe they are acting as parasites on society, while corporate executives who provide no societal value are hailed as great successes. A 2010 study showed that executives, managers, supervisors, and financial professionals account for about 60 percent of the top 0.1 percent of income earners in the US in recent years[26]. In a system where all work was directly tied to the product or service produced, there would be far more societal pressure for people to do something of direct value, and the people contributing nothing would be exposed. With a more open system it would also be far easier for people with current difficulties getting work in the corporate environment to produce something of value.

The internet has always had a strong anti-currency bias. The earliest email spam promotions only served to increase the divide between the corporate world which took over the surface and the underground which remained as before, populated by people derisively referred to as parent's basement dwellers due to the very real truth that their work seldom brought income. The difference between worlds is nowhere more apparent than between Mark Zuckerberg, the billionaire Facebook creator and prodigy of the corporate world, and moot, founder of the most wildly influential, popular and completely unprofitable financially, website 4chan. With no financial incentives, the internet has managed to create collaborative efforts which have pushed the potential of society far beyond what could have been possible before the internet.

While it is doubtful that freeing people to obtain basic essentials outside of corporate bondage would result in more people than usual not working, it is very likely that the increase in art and innovation would be dramatic. It would also change the perception in society of the value of volunteer work if it were necessary and open to everyone to participate in it, and the type of work produced would be valued by society, not corporations. Financial independence is really our term for being able to survive without society. What follows is the idea that if we are independent, our contributions to society are charitable and voluntary. This 'independence' is part of the system of dissociation that stands in our way of creating a real society.

It was once considered inconceivable that the world could run without slavery for the exact same reasons people are now putting forward for retaining wages, our modern slavery.

❯

Heather Marsh

An economy for all

Chapter 25

It is justice, not charity, that is wanting in the world. –
Mary Wollstonecraft

What we are taught to think of as 'the economy' was defined by Aristotle in 350 B.C.E.[27] as the acquisition and use of goods for the household, and expanded to focus on the employment of a small niche group of society who made the accumulation and trading of assets their life's work. 'Productive' labour which adds to the value of materials was recognized, but *"The labour of a menial servant … adds to the value of nothing."* wrote Adam Smith in 1776[28]. After the Industrial Revolution, Karl Marx popularized the inclusion of labour as a commodity when it was expended for the benefit of capitalists and exchanged for a wage[29]. It was separate from the labour of daily life as *"Life for him begins where this activity ceases, at the table, at the tavern, in bed."* Marx pointed out that the exploitation of waged labour was the ultimate source of profit and surplus value in capitalism.

While it was recognized at this point that workers and slaves in capitalist industry were important parts of the economy and were exploited by capitalism, all work done in support of the household and community became invisible. The exploitation of the household and community labourer was the ultimate source of profit and surplus value in waged labour. The exclusion of this labour was perhaps understandable as able bodied, free men were both the backbone of waged labour and the members of the public with political power. According to what Mary Wollstonecraft called *"the divine right of husbands"*, women were said to be created for a man's pleasure and service, his children were his property and women were not persons[30]. Their labour was considered rightfully his and their increased labour in his absence not worthy of notice. Marx's masculinist definition of both labour and capitalist exploitation has continued to define both.

The removal of waged workers from the household increased both labour and isolation for the unpaid workers at home and entrenched inequality and patriarchy in households. While it was acknowledged that working for capitalists was exploitation, women in traditional roles were doing what they had always done, so it was said to be natural to them. Exploitation in a marriage and the worker as a capitalist was not considered. Women were taught to be grateful they were shielded from the exploitation of capitalism when they were unpaid workers at home. Equality activists in the 1970's fought briefly to have household work paid by western governments as an acknowledgement of its role in supporting capitalism, but the parallel fight for women to be more widely included in the waged working class was far more immediately successful. Political choice in the west now tends to promote free trade capitalism, nationalist capitalism, or capitalist workers. Any support for society is presented as charity, a luxury not part of an economic system.

Removing women from their role as household and community slaves ought to have created a more balanced and enjoyable society, but instead, it brought far more of the world into the trade economy once occupied by only a small group. As the work

Every society is a continuum of dependencies.

in creating and supporting society has rarely been acknowledged and never been valued, we have gross overproduction and gluttony in trade and extreme poverty in service. Some look at the overproduction in trade goods and speak of a post-scarcity economy, where no one will have to work. Work is not scarce, and never will be. There is always an elderly person to visit and support, a child to care for, a garden to tend, art to create, a world to study or a discussion to participate in. There are homes and communities to be created, other people to advocate for, and goods to create for necessity or pleasure. For some, survival is a full time job, while others need assistance to survive. The time of leisure those working in trade refer to will never exist for those creating and supporting society.

Some feel that the dysfunction caused by a society given over to trade and support of trade will be remedied by including more women in these careers. These people assume women are inherently more caring, giving people, and if, for instance, women were in the military, killing would be a kinder, gentler pastime. This is absurd, as is proven every time women achieve those positions. Men have also proven constantly that they are just as capable of creating and nurturing a society as women are, and prior to the industrial revolution, those were natural roles for them as well. The answer to the dysfunction is not gender balance, but recognition and promotion of the roles that create a rich and rewarding society. Gender balance should be provided by the basic human right to choose one's life's work, but balance will not change the anti-social nature of a trade economy.

Every society is a continuum of dependencies. With the removal of the labour that was supporting this continuum, dependency became another commodity for exploitation by capitalism. People were taught to disregard the societal debt owed for care received at the beginning of their lives, partly as it was not labour with an acknowledged value. As it was formerly considered the natural role of a wife to provide free labour for a husband, it is still considered the natural role of a parent to provide free care for their children. Adults were now considered dissociated from their origins. The propaganda taught that since they didn't ask to be born they owed nothing to society.

Oddly, this lack of obligation for things one didn't ask for did not extend to aging, sickness or disaster. Now it was incumbent on each labourer to hoard the assets they would need for 'independence', a state where they were dissociated from the assistance of society. This 'independence' filled lives with fear, uncertainty and doubt and fed massive insurance and charity industries which provide no real service at all. These industries provide an illusion of independence by blocking and allocating access to societal support that has been present all along such as medical care and assistance from society in emergencies. The independence is false, but the dissociation serves to make some feel entitled and others not. While the trade economy is only possible if the rest of society is doing the creation and support work, society can exist quite well without trade. We have conducted society as a trade relationship to an intolerable degree since international trade became widespread, until it now defines every aspect of society. Capitalism has progressed to the point where only a few control the lives of most of the world, an unsustainable imbalance. We can rewind economy based on trade relationships to a point where many will again benefit from it, by debt jubilee, financial collapse or other, or we can create a new post-industrial economy that benefits all members of society and supports the roles society needs.

Chapter 26

Decentralized trade economies

Peer to peer trading is being increasingly explored as a method to cut out corporate control of the trade economy. Peer to peer trading looks like the illustration below.

Figure 7: Peer to peer

People can trade directly with each other, or through a network, eliminating the central hubs that control distribution and block access of goods. An alternative distribution is the gift economy. It follows a similar diagram but does not involve direct exchange. Instead, goods are given and it is hoped that equivalent goods will be returned.

A common model to discourage freeloading in a gift economy is to require a certain level of contribution from each member. The peer-to-peer / gift economy structure is encouraged as a form of trade suitable to a non-hierarchical society. That depiction is based on an incorrect picture of the society those trading nodes belong to. The difference between a trade relationship and a society with dependencies is obvious to those dependent or unequal in society. Anyone unable to trade an object or act of direct value to a person in power will be left out of a trade network and dependent on charity as shown in the following chart.

The peer to peer model eliminates the corporate hierarchy but leaves the patriarchy alive and well. Peer to peer and gift economies do not allow for society's input to be inherent in the trade transactions. The value of goods traded is rarely created solely by the trader. Some production builds on previous work, some makes use of assets from the commons and some is produced at the expense of work left for others. Some products may violate human rights of others or damage the environment or the society. Trade relationships relate only to negotiations between individuals and do not reflect impact on an entire society.

Power in peer to peer and gift economies is retained by those that control assets. Not only does this not benefit all of the people who historically don't benefit in capitalism, it is easy to see in the following diagram how the cycle will progress right back to where we are today as wealth will again concentrate in those who hoard assets and avoid caring for dependents. Peer to peer trade relationships are simply decentralized capitalism. Bringing that system back to its origins with no change will certainly produce the same result over time which it has produced now.

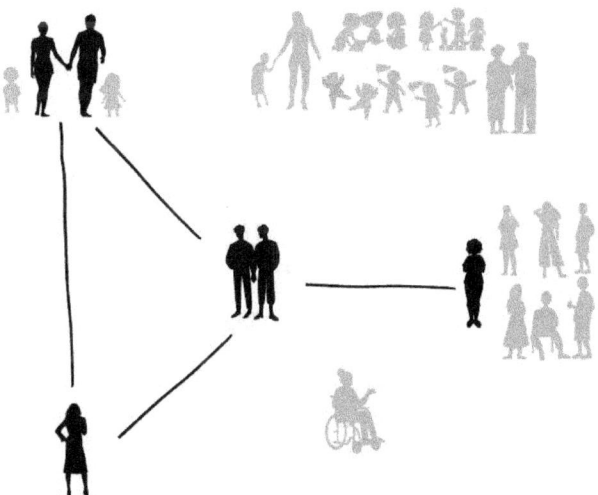

Figure 8: True peer to peer

In the preceding illustration, the two traders who have pooled their resources and have no dependents are the most powerful. The one with six dependents is working far harder and obliged to divide their assets by seven. The disabled individual all by himself, and the one supporting twelve children and two elderly parents cannot participate in the trade economy at all and are dependent on charity. Their needs are not inherent in a trade economy.

For every member of society who has something of outside value to trade, there are dependents who have nothing and others doing the internal society building work. All trade must benefit those powerful enough to reciprocate. People providing palliative or geriatric care, working with the mentally ill or children, or with criminals not participating in the economy, will have no means of survival except charity or a resurrection of the

Slavery of caregivers and others in this and many other instances is the only reason societies under capitalism can survive.

institutional structures described earlier. Those whose own

survival takes all of their available resources because of illness, disability or age, those investing years in a long term project with no observable output, or those working in research and other thought based fields also have no inherent value in a peer to peer structure and must have their needs tacked on as a charitable addendum or debt obligation.

In September 2012, an article appeared in a Canadian newspaper[31]. It told the story of a very young woman in Uganda raising six children, all the product of rape, after being abducted at 13 to become a child soldier. The photojournalist gave her a camera and sold the photos she took with it. When he gave her the money, he said *"This isn't a handout. This is money you've earned."*

Consider that for one minute. Raising six children she did not ask for while still a teenager herself, being pregnant or recovering for six years, breast feeding all of these children for however many years, providing food, shelter, clothing, safety, medical, educational and other care, all 24 hours a day, seven days a week while in extremely dangerous and uncomfortable conditions and recovering from severe trauma, with no societal support and in fact in danger from society, was not worth payment. She is expected to sacrifice her health and risk her life for a job that was not worth payment. Surviving all the trauma of her life did not entitle her to support from society. Trading a picture was considered providing something of value and contributing to society. This is a society conducted as a trade relationship. If she was raising livestock, she would be compensated. She cannot sell her children, therefore her work for them is of no value. It would however be illegal for her to let them die, so she is legally slave labour. Slavery of caregivers and others in this and many other instances is the only reason societies under capitalism can survive.

There are many groups today advocating living a money free existence by using barter, scavenging, peer-to-peer trade and gift economies. Women have been living a money free existence for most of history. Women devote a year of their lives to each pregnancy and recovery period and still do by far the most society building and caregiving work worldwide. In trade economies, they have to add additional labour on top of this to create some product of exchange that will appeal to a person in power or they and all of their dependents will be at the mercy of those in power. The peer-to-peer barter or 'gift' economy required for many to survive has been called the world's oldest profession: prostitution in an endless variety of forms, many called marriage. Trade economies are rigged against women in traditional roles and anyone else creating or supporting society. The answer for equality in this system has been for everyone to reject support roles and embrace trade economies.

Peer to peer networks provide no improvement for the rights of the weak as shown by a history full of peer-to-peer extortion gangs, human trafficking networks and brotherly revolutions which became tyrannical immediately upon seizing power. Peer-to-peer is a survival of the fittest structure which ensures slavery of the weak. The persecution of the weak found in societies without inherent protection is frequently followed by a guardian coup d'état as when women are legally barred from bending over in Swaziland[32], sitting astride motorbikes in Indonesia[33] or owning cell phones in rural India for their own 'protection'[34]. In a society with a trade based economy, currency and centralized power offers more protection to the weak than a peer-to-peer structure. This has been seen by the improvement in women's lives when they have the right to vote and work for pay, and protection is provided (however theoretically) by the state.

When asked how they would allow for dependencies, advocates of peer to peer or gift economies speak of being 'generous', 'giving' food to the less able, and nearly always also mention condemnation for anyone having more children than they can provide for themselves, addictions, etc. In fact, even one child puts the pregnant, nursing and caregiving parent at a huge disadvantage and causes them to have to work far harder, for far less, and then need to divide their earnings. A number of dependents like six or more makes it difficult to survive. Many people around the world have many more than six children as well as care for other dependents in society. Even if the birth rate were reduced, every state in the northern hemisphere is experiencing an explosion in the elderly population, and disasters, environmental harm and other factors can cause sudden huge increases in dependents.

The decentralized capitalist structures treat this 'problem', in very much the same way as their corporate capitalist predecessors, with a begrudging charity or more hostile superiority and blame for those disadvantaged by their system. The value attached to trade versus creation and support of society is evident in every part of life, from obnoxious business travelers and others treating child caregivers as an untouchable caste to the removal of the elderly and less able to a dependent, burdensome role instead of recognizing the contributions and effort they are still providing or could. The nostalgia for a time before rampant corporate capitalism took hold, when 'everyone' benefited from peer-to-peer trade is an entirely masculinist view with a very narrow definition of 'everyone'. As the male role in society has expanded to include far more caregiving, a trade economy suits no one.

Societies have never been shy about dictating what type of person should become a mother or the behaviour expected once someone becomes a mother, but these pressures are not shared by the rest of society. While the mother is expected to be an impossible paragon, modern societies feel no obligation to provide a safe and welcoming, educational and nurturing environment. A mother that does not love her child is considered an abomination. A society that does not love its children is considered natural and justified.

The right to have children or not is an individual right of women only. The children, once born, are the responsibility of society, primarily through support of parenthood. In modern society, people are no longer accustomed to the idea that they are responsible to a society of people. While they will easily accept responsibility for a road that they may or may not use, a person without children has been taught to feel robbed by responsibility for a school. In a society of plenty, children are no longer presented as the support of the future but simply as the burden of the present.

People are paid to kill, not to give birth. While the right to suicide is contested, the responsibility to provide care for the elderly and ill while they choose to live is not up for debate. They are not told that since the choice to live is theirs, the responsibility must also be fully theirs. Society accepts that adults have the right to choose whether to live and yet is willing to support their life. Society does not fully accept that women have the right to give birth (or not) and yet places full responsibility for the child on the woman who gives birth.

Chapter 27

Exploitation of dependents as a commodity

In a world where everything is bought and sold, the weak become the product.

The elderly are taught to live in fear of outliving their rights to care or even a home and food, and the pressure to hoard everything for the time when they can no longer work hangs over the lives of every worker. Since no one can know when they will become ill, when they will die, or what the vagaries of the financial system will bring, this stress colours the lives of everyone in society and makes generosity with any current surplus unlikely.

Insurance corporations which provide nothing of real value to society have sprung up for every eventuality and advertise potential calamity incessantly. The fearful society then buys insurance instead of using their surplus to help others experiencing a current disaster. Sometimes this protection racket is mandated by law and it is impossible to drive a car, mortgage a house or other activities without paying an insurance company selling fear.

Sickness is controlled not only by the insurance companies but by the health industry which controls choice. The wealthy can afford real health solutions in the form of healthy lifestyles and expensive testing, counseling, therapy and remedies. The poor are either denied health care or fed the most harmful and invasive quick-fix pharmaceuticals and procedures with little to no after care or general wellness assistance. Poor health is considered an individual responsibility despite frequently or usually being caused by societal pollution, poor nutritional options, unsafe environments, etc.

Caregivers are threatened with no hope for their child's future if they are not provided with an endless array of products and services tiered by income to determine future status in society. The education caregivers are convinced is necessary for a child to succeed is only necessary to perpetuate the trade economy. The poor are streamed to schools which teach the futility of resistance[35] and the reality that elite options will never be available[36] to them. The wealthy are taught to excel in arts, athletics and academics to no purpose except to appear accomplished in the manner of the old aristocracy. Character and how to benefit the society they are born into, the topics which may be expected to be the only necessary topics for a state education, are almost never taught.

Young adults are persuaded they must mortgage their futures before beginning them by entering overwhelming debt agreements for education which benefits the trade economy. Jobs in labour are frequently sold in a similar manner[37]. Governments or agents charge fees for emigrating labour which ensures they will be enslaved by the purchased job for years. This ensures workers can never leave the trade economy as they are indentured for years, captured first by paying for the privilege of working, second by fears for retirement.

However reasonable a legal system may seem, lawyers and an arbitrary system of judicial discretion ensure that the laws work against the poor. It does not matter if the law is on the side of the poor if a rich opponent drags the process out for years and bankrupts them, or ensures they cannot keep up with the legal process or they do not have the expertise or time to fight. Civil courts have succeeded for years in destroying the lives of those the law should have protected by protracted lawsuits and exorbitant fees. Now many countries are seeing pre-trial detentions[38] abused in the same manner and prisoners denied their rights to a speedy trial.

Once in prison, people become part of a huge predatory industry. Taxes pay private or state owned corporations set up to warehouse prisoners, not rehabilitate them. Many prisons worldwide have the added feature of penal labour where prisoners are paid far below minimum wage and their services sold to other corporations at a great discount[39]. Taxpayers pay to feed and house people who are forced to work as slaves for corporations. There is no incentive in a trade economy to not build and fill as many prisons as possible.

Disasters which require voluntary assistance are preyed upon by NGO's who build powerful empires by standing between those in need and the society willing to help them[40]. 'Rebuilding' efforts are typically an opportunity for multinational corporations to come in and exploit the disaster site with offers of 'creating jobs'[41]. Disaster NGO's use money provided by people around the world to support huge industries of developers, security, and disaster relief.

Political unrest supports the global war industry. Once, a peace agreement generally meant disarmament[42]. Now when 'peace' finally arrives to a region, after extended media advertisements of all the war equipment being used, extensive new mass killing equipment[43] is purchased to 'ensure peace'. The end of a war, like every other disaster, is a signal for the 'rebuilding' efforts of NGO empires and exploitative multi-nationals[44].

Wide spread and growing human trafficking is a product of a society built on trade relationships[45]. Preying particularly on the weakest members of society, human traffickers also frequent disaster areas looking for those who will not be easily traced. People are captured and sold for slavery[46], including rape slavery[47], child rape[48], military,[49] organ harvesting[50] and even ritual killings[51] where their body parts are said to bring wealth and power to the purchaser.

The poor are exploited by capitalism through uncountable fees, fines, and price gouging. When they receive money it is subject to a vast array of charges from the financial industry, for cashing cheques, fines for missed payments, interest on debt, and a wide assortment of tiered services such as credit cards which are impossibly expensive for the poor but provide benefits to the rich. Stores will raise the prices of essentials on days when benefits are paid to ensure the poor pay more. In many cases poor people are expected to 'volunteer' in exchange for food or lodging in yet another form of modern slavery. Frequently the lifestyle forced by poverty leaves no legal choices and forces them into the prison system.

In a trade economy, dependency is a product to be exploited and sold to society for maximum profit.

Chapter 28

Approval economy

To benefit all of society, an economy needs to be based on service to all of society. In today's economy, service is bought and sold as a good. Instead goods must be provided as a service. An economy benefitting all of society should include service to ourselves, service to others and service to society at large. An elderly person who keeps themselves healthy and fulfilled or an addict working to conquer their addiction may be giving only to themselves, but both are making society a much better place and lessening the work for others. To create a giving economy instead of a gift economy, exchange is not between two trading partners. Societal approval is awarded from all of society to the giver. Societal approval and trust then entitles each member of a society to receive benefit from that society, through a living and immediate social contract. As a reputation economy allows you to participate in trade, an approval economy allows you to become part of a society.

Trade economies attempt to symbolically represent societal approval by possessions. As monarchs were formerly held to rule by divine right, trade economies insist wealth is due to virtue. While hoarded possessions have been used as a symbol of acceptance, they do not fulfill the real social need for acceptance. The wealthy are instead resented and isolated, shunned by the society they supposedly are the elite members of. Underlying every patriarchal society is the idea that caregivers, children and dependents should be grateful as trade economies see them as burdensome. Those who see a disparity in labour for the family and community are not at all grateful. Wage earners resent not gaining love and approval for their work in trade but because trade economy derides unpaid service, they receive no respect for support and creation of the society either. In a trade economy, the currency exchanged separates the giver and receiver. Because the currency entitles the receiver to the gift they are not grateful. The human need for social and familial approval is almost never adequately met in trade economies.

As possessions in a trade economy include the service of others, those who do not work for the benefit of others are the powerful. An economy based on societal approval equates not working for others with being excluded or shunned. In an approval based economy, control of assets does not bring power. Assets are not assigned worth until they are contributed to the society. Internal support contributions are not valued less than external trade contributions.

Work in an approval based economy provides society and affinity groups. It is less stressful to be part of the society than to be isolated. Gifts are bonding, both within family and friends and at a community level. In an approval economy gifts are not a tax or state confiscation which leaves nothing. Wealth is created by giving. Acceptance by society is based on actions instead of assets. Those dependent in society for some things also have gifts to give, acceptance and approval being the most valuable. Politicians propped up by military and corporate interests hated by the people are the antithesis of social approval as the mark of acceptance. The dissociation of power in society from service to society provides fertile ground for sociopaths to seize power.

Those creating and supporting society should not need charity, they should have power. An inclusive society does not leave some dependent on the charity of others, or make some work far harder for the same ends. Where there is inequality there will always be tyrants. Giving birth, aging or accepting responsibility for another should not be equivalent to accepting a slave role. 'Women's issues', the elderly, the youth and the less able cannot be special problems to be dealt with on the fringes of society. Care for dependents of society is the responsibility of all, and dependents should have power to gift approval to those who assist them. Economy cannot be rigged to favour one special interest group. The solutions for all of society must be inherent within the economic system. In an approval economy, effort to benefit society is recognized and acts against society are penalized. Approval is related to assessment of fairness, not the value of the gift. The work of an elderly person talking to a child, a scientist conducting research, a maker providing goods, a child learning and a mentally less able person gardening have no value differences, though the effort expended might.

In the following image, the person with a score of 91 has decided to be a pillar of their society. They probably belong to few other societies, and devote formidable energy to providing for this one, belonging to many working and discussion groups and making themselves available and responsible for the well being of others. The people scored 58 and 52 may be just visiting or may belong to many networks, or perhaps they prefer to spend their days on the beach, doing only the basic amount necessary for good standing. They may be entitled to basic essentials like food and lodging but not community resources such as cars and maker labs without additional barter. The people at 55 and 50 expend effort, but also cause harm. Perhaps they are struggling with addiction or mental illness. Their effort is recognized by continued support but at basic levels to restrict their ability to harm others. The person scored at 15 is probably completely shunned by the society, perhaps even imprisoned.

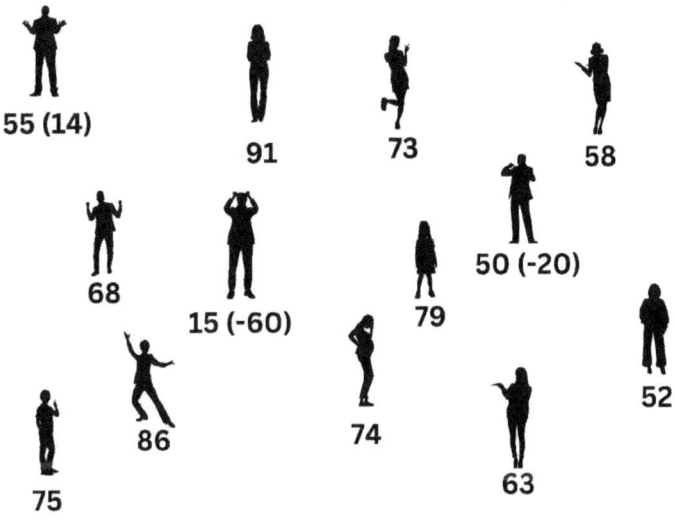

Figure 9: Approval economy

An approval economy is the economy people rely on when they do not use direct coercion, the one typically seen in families and unfunded cooperative and volunteer groups. What the approval ratings mean in terms of benefits earned and whether there are formal values at all varies by society. Being part of a society may require more effort at some times than at others. For instance, not assisting to put out a fire or provide emergency aid to another may be considered an act against society rather than simply a failure to contribute. The benefits of belonging to a society will dictate how motivated people are to contribute to it.

Chapter 29

Acceptance and shunning

Acts which cost society should reduce the standing of the destroyer and their access to benefits. Theft reduces the thief's approval which is their wealth. Acts of aggression against society is reflected back to harm the aggressor's standing and remove power and privilege. Extreme aggression in violation of the social contract results in shunning, or removal from the benefits of society. Every person has a right to belong to a society except in extreme cases as complete shunning can be equivalent to a death sentence. Law enforcement by shunning is inherent in a system of trust networks. In dissociated trade economies, criminals are allowed to fully participate in society until a point when they are completely removed from society. Societal approval and rehabilitation have nothing to do with punishment in a trade economy. Far from being shunned, many criminals are media celebrities or enjoy wide-spread societal support.

Acceptance or reintegration into society in an approval economy is a product of subsequent good behaviour and effort expended to increase approval. A person who has lost their good standing would be forced into a trade economy relationship to receive any benefits and have to 'pay up front' rather than have the rights of a member of society. Shunning would ensure that laws were true reflections of popular opinion, though shunning must never be used to remove the rights in a social contract by mob rule.

Societies can join in expanded networks which may agree to trust individual reputations across the network. These networks can also agree to shun other societies they do not approve of or assist those they do. Those societies that do not join expanded networks do not receive the benefits of them. People that have good standing across multiple networks can increase their standing in each by providing referrals and knowledge, or some networks might agree to blend rankings to create an

Approval economies are the natural economies of human society.

overall reputation. In this way, people who do not work locally can still access the essentials they need locally. An expanded network would also provide an avenue of appeal if a person felt their local society was shunning them unjustly or they were having their basic human rights violated. Expanded networks which create apartheid would violate basic human rights which must be considered above the rights of any group.

The trust networks and reputations which make up an approval economy are part of the daily life of all societies already. The people you invite to eat a dinner you have provided are typically people who have earned your trust and approval. They will usually provide similar benefits to you if they are able, and if they consistently do not, they may begin to receive less invitations. We care for grandparents who are unable to reciprocate because we recognize ourselves as part of a continuum of family obligation which cared for us when we were young and will hopefully do so again when we are old. When we ask the identity of an absent group member, their reputation and approval rating is frequently implied in the answer, and sometimes we ask for referrals outright. Even as anonymous participants on some internet sites our input is ranked and voted up and down, contributing to our reputation. Sometimes our internet reputation is already used to introduce us to wider societies providing basic needs, such as couchsurfing.

Approval economies are the natural economies of human society. We separated power from societal approval and exchanged society for trade relationships so long ago most cannot imagine an alternative, but it is still there in the most basic units of society. Economies based on trade relationships with financial systems as tools of coercion and control cannot coexist with peaceful and just societies. Power will be concentrated in able bodied traders and hoarders as long as we continue using trade economies.

Beyond nation states

Chapter 30

Governments now are run by hierarchical groups which act as the final authority on all topics for an entire region for an arbitrarily specified length of time or until they are overthrown by another group. What these authorities govern is a series of systems, controlled by the state or corporations. Systems covering everything from health care to community infrastructure have profit and control for the top of the hierarchy as their objectives. They are not set up to provide an efficient or superior service or product to the users. They do not accept input from the users in any meaningful manner. Currently, voters elect representatives by regional boundaries, but in reality, most decisions and actions are taken by ministries or private corporations divided by function, not region. If each system was governed by its own user group, every person would belong to many overlapping or separate systems, each with their own culture and governance, similar to the different levels of regional governance now.

The current political structure does not recognize that every system is not of concern or interest to everyone in the region or that many systems are of far wider concern than one state. We need responsibility and control (governance and ownership) to rest with the entire user group and functionality for the entire user group, not profit or power, should be the objective. If individual rights and the rights of global commons are accepted as being paramount, every user group should, subject only to these conditions, be entitled to govern themselves. Each user group should consist of all people affected by the system and no people not affected by the system. The debate around who the user group of each system is would be the most challenging aspect of this type of governance.

Contribution at all levels of each system must be open to all users. Expertise can be assessed and acquired in concentric user groups, and work can be contributed and accepted or rejected by stigmergy. Having all German federal law and regulations on Github is a great idea, but only if pull requests are allowed from the people affected by the laws of Germany. An open working group allows people to work on anything they like. They are not required to submit resumes and acquire accreditation, seniority, or approval from an individual authority. If their work is good enough it will be accepted by the user group. Everyone can work on the system that interests them, doing the jobs at the level they are capable of, with as much or as little involvement as they choose. If the worker is also part of the user group, the benefits to themselves are immediate and obvious. The most effective way to prevent producer and consumer conflict of interests is to eliminate separation between the two. The farmer who eats their own food has an interest in producing healthy food.

All information related to the system must be fully transparent in order for users to participate in tasks or auditing and to learn how to contribute. Transparency allows every user of the system to explain to anyone interested what is being developed and why, how to contribute and any other information new users require. Transparency allows users to act as the knowledge bridges to train new users.

Some people seeking new economic alternatives are pushing to have ownership of property abolished or severely restricted. It is, of course, completely within the power of a society to remove property from individuals, corporations or anyone else and also to change the laws which allowed property ownership. It has certainly been done before many times in past societies. Like oligarchies, property ownership does not tend to stay away when it is removed. Usually, ownership removed from an individual is transferred to a group. To see the problems inherent in this, we only need to look back at the problems with corporatist groups and hidden oligarchies. These issues with abolishing ownership have been demonstrated in the past by many alternative societies which battled cult leaders attempting to seize ownership or control of surrendered property.

Property ownership, defined as rights to property, always exists. Abolishing property ownership only hides it. Ownership as the right to possess, preserve, rent, sell, use, give away, or destroy property most logically accompanies governance as a right of the user group. Governance as the decision making and management of a system by those with the right to do so and property ownership defined as the rights and responsibilities associated with specific property are used interchangeably here as they ought to be inseparable.

Property ownership causes problems when control of property is held outside of the user group. When a community owns an individual's home, an individual owns a community's public space, or a state lays claim to an ocean, problems are inevitable.

Chapter 31

Personal integrity

In order to create a healthy society which can reach its full potential, we must start with healthy individuals who can reach their full potential. Each person ought to have ownership and authority over all matters which affect only their own person. This is not simple.

Each person has the right to control over their own body. Illness can sometimes change the functioning of a brain and cause a person to make decisions they would not have made before the illness. Which then is the official authority to reference, what is the point at which a person loses their own decision making ability, who makes that decision and who then takes control of decision making for that body?

Sometimes a body is shared by two or more identities. Rarely in the case of conjoined twins and frequently in the case of pregnancy, two lives are affected by the decisions over one body.

In the case of pregnancy, a commonly held view in countries with legal abortion is that both lives are the mother's to control until the fetus is capable of autonomous life. Some will argue that only the pregnant woman is entitled to an opinion and others that the unborn child also has rights. Still others will argue the loss of a potential child in the future gives the father or society a vote as well. If the child has rights over the body, is the mother guilty of attempted murder if she attempts suicide? Negligence if she has a car accident? If so, is she also negligent for lifestyle choices before pregnancy which may have damaged eggs? What if the pregnancy was accidental? And is the father also negligent for unhealthy sperm? For those who feel the mother never has the right to terminate a pregnancy, even if her life is at risk, how does the fetus then have the right to terminate the mother's life? What are the start and end points of life in the timeline between potential conception and potential resurrection?

Many answers to these questions will have to rely in large part on what the underlying principles of individual rights are accepted to be. These are decisions which will have to be defined in the social contract of each society. If a society decides abortion is solely a woman's choice, it would be impossible to then argue that a state could require women to have an internal ultrasound prior to the abortion. If the situation is defined as within her user group only, then only she makes all of the decisions for it.

No one can own another person. Human trafficking and all forms of the slave trade have been considered abhorrent all over the world for years. A child requires special care as they cannot be autonomous at birth. If the parents do not own the child, what is it that gives them more right than another to raise the child? Is there a separate social contract that applies to members of a family where they agree to care for each other ahead of the rest of society? It would make sense to think of each person as belonging to many societies, some small enough to be considered relationships, others large enough to encompass all of earth or the universe. Each society would have its own agreement of mutual obligations, dependency and respect, forming its own social contract.

Living life to its full potential does entail taking risks. A society that promises to remove all insecurity is crippling the freedom and challenge required to reach full potential. Personal risk is personal choice, until responsibility for the repercussions of that risk fall on the rest of society. Consumption of drugs alone is a personal decision; consumption of drugs while driving a vehicle in public involves everyone who may be harmed. Consumption of drugs in the home may also involve other people in the home, and health systems the drug user relies on may have input as well.

The right to defend oneself is found in a state of nature, but freedom from living life as prey is a primary motivation for leaving a state of nature to enter society. The physical reaction of fear, revulsion and stress from being stalked or under constant threat does not allow for the peace of mind necessary for freedom. If a society is beneficial, its role is to protect each member against, not just violent assault, but also the constant threat and reasonable fear of assault. When the right to defend overwhelms the right to feel secure a society is at war with itself and not functioning as a refuge.

The right for freedom of expression or action stops being an individual decision at the point where it harms the freedom of another. Free speech when used to prevent or inhibit the speech of another becomes censorship. State censorship interferes with freedom of speech for all, but hate speech primarily attacks only vulnerable groups. The right to

The right for freedom of expression or action stops being an individual decision at the point where it harms the freedom of another.

produce and broadcast violence has been allowed to overwhelm the right of vulnerable populations to feel secure. In most countries, propaganda against vulnerable groups has caused violence, and in some, it has even caused attempted genocide. In the past, the right to 'freedom of the press' has been forced on sovereign states so that wealthy foreign press can overwhelm the society with foreign propaganda. This can serve as a form of censorship by misinformation and noise, drowning out the voices of others. Social media has provided an effective counter to such attempts lately and is beginning to regulate censorship by hate speech as well.

Invasion of privacy has been conveniently defined by groups such as reddit administrators and moderators to protect the names of men posting creepshots but not the naked bodies of women and children posted to the website. The rights of paparazzi to freedom of speech have been allowed to completely overwhelm the rights of women with public jobs to privacy or security. This also infringes on women's freedom of speech and ability to pursue power. The right to information about actions which affect the public has been transformed into the right to invade the privacy of any person the media deems newsworthy. Revenge porn and creep shots imply ownership of the woman, child abuse media violates the dignity of the child. The reaction of paparazzi defending their creep shots of Kate Middleton by saying she should not be 'ashamed of her body' denied her ownership and authority over her own privacy. Those who argue that simply viewing child rape or exploitation or other unwilling porn does no harm are denying the harm of a violation to privacy.

Privacy and ownership of personal stories are closely related to human dignity. Violation of these rights is commonly associated with degradation and humiliation. The importance of these rights to our well-being is highlighted by the number of suicides among people humiliated by gossip or other invasions of their human dignity and by the existence of shame as a human emotion. The difference between rape and any other physical assault is this added violation. When authoritarians attempt to humiliate those they seek control over, they violate ownership and authority in these areas. We see this more and more as states demand greater control, starting with strip searches and 'cavity searches' (rape) of vulnerable populations like prisoners and now widespread to the general population of the world.

The public side of personal stories is reputation, an intangible possession of great value to humans. While jealousy and pride are not generally considered virtues, they are essential motivators and guides to a person's behaviour. Pride and shame are the built-in methods of coercion societies use to encourage certain types of behaviour in people. All that goes into a person's reputation contributes to their acceptance and approval in society. Societal approval is a far more powerful tool of governance than military might. A person must have the right to protect their reputation from unwarranted malice or theft as it is used to purchase their acceptance in society.

While individual rights applied equally for all is a sufficient principle in some cases, sometimes there are conflicting priorities and needs. Each of these situations is open to endless nuance and it must be the choice of local governance to define their own customs. Individual rights need to ensure consideration and respect for all. Those that are decrepit or ill, those that are not fully matured, those that can give birth, those that are raising children or are in other ways directly responsible for the well being of others must be protected as well as the general population without special interest groups having to form and lobby for their voices to be amplified. In defining all rights, special care must be taken that those rights will not infringe on the rights of others. In this way systems which respect individual rights can operate autonomously knowing they are causing no harm to others.

Chapter 32

Personal property

I t is sometimes extremely hard to separate people from their childhood blanket, favourite shirt, or in adulthood, first car, and ultimately home. History shows a natural trait of humans, like ravens, to become bonded with physical objects. There is commonly felt delight in finding and creating objects, and many people have keepsakes that they use to trigger memories of a loved person, time or place. There is also commonly felt jealousy and clashes over possessions. In some people, an attachment to possessions can become a crippling disorder. Others have managed to forsake all feelings of attachment. It is difficult to generalize to what extent possessions may be tied to happiness, but it is readily apparent that almost all people possess more objects than they can easily care for, and the ownership causes more stress than contentment.

Personal property must be considered a natural right as few mammals will not feel they are attacked if their property (such as food and shelter) is taken. The right to personal property has been enshrined in almost every political system and body of law as well as in the Universal Declaration of Human Rights, Article 17, and in the European Convention on Human Rights, Protocol 1. John Locke went as far as to say *"The reason why men enter into society is the preservation of their property"*[52] and The Communist Manifesto allowed *"hard-won, self-acquired, self-earned"*[53] property not based on the labour of others.

If a society agrees that slavery must not exist then property as a result of labour can only belong to the labourer. A gift of labour to the community must then result in approval and enhanced reputation and acceptance for the labourer, not any other group or individual. The right to ownership or credit for the results of labour may be considered a right of personal integrity as it contributes to reputation and societal approval. Societal approval is not just a basic need of all humans, it may be an economic necessity in an approval based economy. Credit or property ownership unclaimed does not disperse. We have proven it goes to feed a form of capitalism where all unclaimed credit or property will feed an oligarch. The safest way to avoid such unjust oligarchy is to simply leave credit or ownership in the place they originate and trust the lure of societal approval to encourage sharing of surplus. Appropriate credit allocation is part of transparency and information the public needs in order to govern themselves.

Personal property can at times extend to body parts or enhancements in which case the sole user group is the person wearing or using the property. If ownership is by user group they must also be the owner. Property such as shelter may be tied to personal security and also have a sole user. These possessions only create conflict if they are scarce and deplete community resources until there is not equivalent property available for all. Property acquired by labour may also use scarce resources in the case of a garden or similar enhanced value. The allocation of scarce property must be a decision for local governance and would probably be tied to either societal approval or relative need. The homesteading principle of ownership by the first person to claim a property implies that earlier ownership did not exist. Ownership always exists; unclaimed property belongs to the commons. Ownership must then be given by the user group of the commons, not seized. The same applies to intangible property such as concepts. It is for the user group to decide who to allocate credit to, not for an individual to file copyright or patent claims.

An antipathy to gluttony and waste is a fairly universal feeling which most of the world is ignoring. Creation can bring great joy and fulfillment, but overproduction of goods encourages people to destroy and waste their property instead of becoming attached to it. If personal property is the result of either the owner's labour or a gift from someone it is far less likely to be wasted or overproduced. In a system where the essentials of life are provided for free and there is no need for people to perform work that does not appeal to them, it is likely that few will elect to make maintenance of another's assets their life's work. If maintenance of assets becomes the sole responsibility of the owner, excessive property ownership will quickly become a burden instead of a privilege. If each person is allocated the right to dispose of only a limited amount of waste, it would also curb overproduction.

The world today combines the ability to easily provide basic essentials for everyone on earth with very little labour and an unprecedented ability to live lightly. A room full of stereo equipment, libraries full of books, precious family photos and papers, legal documentation, letters, banks and so much more are all accessible from a borrowed smart phone. With very few items that are either precious or uncommon, in the way that a book before the printing press was both precious and uncommon, or cloth before looms, acquiring, hoarding and guarding property seems more and more a futile vocation.

In response to any anti-consumer revulsion, there are policies of forced ownership in some countries, especially in North America. Insurance and liability which discourage sharing, a refusal to build bike lanes or provide reasonable public transit, and 'safety standards' which require the constant disposal of perfectly functioning assets, even including items as large as houses and cars, overcome our natural antipathy to waste.

Children are given lifelong back injuries to ensure that they continue to buy paper and books instead of putting their school supplies on a tablet. Families are threatened with the loss of their children if they do not live in a house deemed large enough and built with all of the government required features. People are forbidden to share their accommodation with others by a variety of regulations at all levels of government. Food which cannot be used by stores and restaurants is poisoned with bleach rather than let it be used by freegans or food banks. Many laws are now being attempted which prevent the growing, preparing, or sharing of food by anyone 'unlicensed' or inhibit the ability of people to provide this basic need for themselves or others. Desperate advertising is needed to continue to convince people they need possessions which simply burden them.

Not following the natural impulse of attachment to material goods creates a disposable culture that humans are not naturally comfortable with. From the moment the first human picked up a rock and took it home to play with or share, we have been attached to inanimate objects. We like to create, and gift giving cultures world wide have evolved with the delight of sharing material property. Corporate culture has served to separate people from their attachment to objects, to encourage hoarding as an ownership culture instead of a sharing one, and to devalue property by a glut of goods.

With greater internet communication, people are connecting cerebrally around ideas and traveling more to meet more people outside of their economic circles. Here economic disparity introduces awkwardness and is a barrier unless sharing becomes part of the expected behaviour in the circle. It is not enjoyable to have what your peers cannot. The ability to drive to a restaurant and eat an expensive meal by yourself while your friends are all making dinner in a park does not allow for the social life which most people crave. For many years, the solution to this dilemma was to create societies based on corresponding wealth. Within each physical location, the very rich built guarded fortresses and they created enclaves for shopping, eating, living etc., which only they could afford. This way they are not put to the discomfort of being economically isolated from the rest of their community.

As the economic disparity grows wider, the need for stronger barricades and greater isolation of the enclaves increases. As the numbers of very poor increase and very rich decrease, and as the middle class buffer of sycophants and servants disappears, the isolation and paranoia in the very rich will add to the pressure and decrease the attractiveness of belonging to this society. While some may simply build higher walls, others are likely to question their society and explore more attractive alternatives.

Chapter 33

Community commons

Today's so-called nation states are nothing of the sort. They are economic markets designed to ensure unequal distribution of wealth. No state is now a pure nation by ethnicity, religious belief, or any other common factor except economic opportunity. Moving from one state to another is no longer a significant cultural journey. Nations in a pure sense do not exist. When state leaders speak of 'our values' it is a meaningless phrase since every state now has diverse values. 'Our way of life' is a far more honest description.

Society is built not by ethnic origin or citizenship but by shared values outlined in a social contract. Any society should be free to join by any individual who agrees to abide by the social contract. A political structure which rejects discrimination based on racism, sexism, ageism, and all other forms of collective shunning yet embraces nationalism is overdue for collapse. An apartheid world is no more logical, sustainable or moral than an apartheid state.

If communities were organized by society, there would be no need for militant policing of borders as there is when they are organized by economic opportunity. It would be far easier for a society to reach consensus on shared values and a social contract if they were already arranged by affinity group. Our current system of dividing people by land mass ensures we will never be able to govern by consensus and must have the warring political parties and win/lose governance of representative or direct democracy. Acceptance of a social contract would be a true acceptance if our naturally migratory species had the right to join whatever society or societies best suited them. There would be no need for external forces to protect human rights if every society was open to be left or joined. No person should be subjected to the law of a society whose social contract they did not accept; they can only be shunned from that society. No child must be subjected to the laws of the social contract unless they have reached an age of informed acceptance.

Acceptance of a social contract means it is not collective punishment if that society is shunned by others. When sanctions are applied to economic regions by land mass, as they are to Iran, North Korea and Cuba, it is collective punishment and a war crime. Global pressure on societies is far more reasonable if they have willingly accepted the values the rest of the world objects to.

Governance by society would allow the adoption of methods and principles not in common use today. Alternative economic systems or living structures could be explored in small communities and the ones that appeared attractive would spread to other societies. The world would not need to all adhere to the same methods and principles except in matters involving other communities.

These societies do not need to lead to segregation. A society does not need to be connected by land mass. There is no reason why multiple societies cannot share resources and economic communities or locations as long as their principles do not conflict. As we currently have different religions living in the same community, we can have other different societies in the same community. Societies which adopt principles in conflict with generally held views would be shunned. Communal property such as resources ought to belong to the entire user group and it would be subject to it's own rules of governance.

Each person could and would belong to many different societies. They may belong to a family group, a local economic group, an international economic group and a religion. They may contribute to a community garden, a global epistemic community, a local news network and a football club. They may access a local commons, an international network of local commons, and the global commons. Their standing in each community is unaffected by the other communities except where they agree to form networks for economic or other purposes. This is actually exactly how we govern ourselves now in most of our daily life. Every family group has its own social contract, we all belong to community, international and global user groups, and we all access the local and global commons. This is a picture of society as it exists in reality, without the arbitrary and unnecessary state cages.

Figure 10: Real society

Gun control laws in Arctic Canada dictated through state democracy by people in Toronto, Montreal and Vancouver, would be illogical and unfair. The concerns of people in those cities would need to be considered regarding any weapons that were brought within range of causing harm to the people there, but communities would decide local matters for themselves. Drilling for oil in the Arctic is at the other end of the spectrum, and for one or a group of nations or corporations to assert a 'right' to drill for oil in the Arctic, dump iron fertilizer and radioactive material into the Pacific or oil and dispersants into the Atlantic is a violation of the rights of the global commons. Oceans do not even belong to one generation much less one species, one state or one corporation.

If we had governance by user group, and every user group was open to anyone who agreed to community consensus, there would be no purpose for states. Instead of being governed in arbitrary boxes by land mass, we would be able to travel freely among overlapping rings by function.

In environmentally sensitive areas such as the Arctic, the few who live in the area must have their rights considered along with the rights of the planet. A balance needs to be struck between the needs of the local population, who may, for instance, require (or choose) a seal hunt to ensure the fish population or seal products they need to survive, and the rights of the planet which is not particularly affected by it. The opinion of the people in the rest of the world who may be revolted by the seal hunt must not be allowed to override the needs or wishes of those who live there unless they can prove actual longterm negative impact to the environment. The solution for those revolted would be found in trade relationships they may choose to terminate or communication to present their position.

Each local user group or individual should have access to outside user groups for trade, shared knowledge, disaster relief, etc., autonomous but networked into a larger society for mutual support.

Chapter 34

Global commons

Anything which is not only of global interest but also does not belong to any one generation cannot legitimately be claimed as the property of any individual, group, corporation or government. Global commons would include space, the atmosphere and electromagnetic field, deep sea ocean, land and water masses of sufficient size to have global impact, areas of the biosphere which are rare or important enough to be of global concern, and knowledge. Knowledge includes discoveries, history, creative works, and the information people require in order to govern themselves and excludes personal information regarding individuals. If society is to progress, there should be no restriction on the use of ideas.

Anything belonging to the global commons should be held under stewardship of a permeable and transparent organization set up for the purpose and under the scrutiny of all. The mandate for all global commons must include the protection and preservation of the commons. The Public Trust Doctrine by Emperor Justinius declared in 529 A.D. *"By the laws of nature, these things are common to all mankind: the air, running water, the sea and consequently the shores of the sea."*[54] England's Charter of the Forest is the foundation for many rights documents in the English speaking world.[55] It demanded protection of a commons for fuel, food and construction of shelter, all that was essential for life. This type of commons is set up to preserve the means for every person to attain their basic human rights of shelter and food. This idea of a global commons has been reinforced many times in many cultures and was considered self evident in earlier history.

Some people are now taking the idea of a global commons further to include the rights of the environment as separate and above its use to humans. The integrity of the earth, water and all species is considered not just as a source of human needs but as having inherent rights of its own. The 2008 Constitution of Ecuador with its Rights of Nature and Bolivia's 2010 Law of the Rights of Mother Earth are two recent attempts to codify those rights. Like individual rights, the needs of the global commons must take precedence over all user groups.

Corporations have now claimed the right to destroy environments above the political authority of regional governance. This has been seen repeatedly as resource corporations sue in international courts for their 'right' to destroy environments and livelihoods against the wishes of communities. People are held accountable for contracts, treaties and laws that representative governance has enabled far above their heads. Security contractors are hired to violently enforce these supposedly binding contracts the people were not party to. States and multinational bodies have taken so-called representative governance to mean ownership of the basic rights of the people. Corporations as superhuman embodiments of their usually foreign based owners could not possibly be said to have a legitimate interest in the resources of a community.

Because of the arbitrary political division into states, governments of the world have been allowed to act as though they were not responsible for the results of their actions felt outside their own borders. The reality of a global commons, where the actions of one depletes the opportunity of others, is illustrated in the climate debts from the global north to the global south. Both the damage to their environments and the loss of their fair share of the atmospheric space they now cannot use if climate change is to be stopped are debts the south logically claim against the north.

Chapter 35

Intangible property

Education must be free to allow everyone to achieve their full potential. Right now education is seen as part of a competitive society where more educated people are competition for scarce jobs. Once, family secrets were used to ensure economic advantage. Old family recipes and other domestic skills made women more marketable as wives in the same manner that possession of trade secrets made men in trade more marketable. These trade secrets are no longer necessary on a personal basis and are now used by corporations. In a stigmergic workplace and an approval based economy, the success of one does not deplete the success of another. If all individuals are at liberty to achieve their full potential, society will be far richer for their contributions.

The lack of free knowledge is crippling progress. Because no one can build on ideas that work and all must start from a different point, we lose a great deal of innovation and research speed. In the case of diseases, environmental health and other urgent crises, we cannot afford the loss in time or the added expense and inaccessibility brought by idea ownership.

While the scientific community theoretically embraces open-source principles, in practice, knowledge production is done in private because of the competition to produce papers and gain research funding. There is no incentive to publish ideas and half researched papers that one has no time or inclination to finish. Ideas are not released for the research to be crowd sourced by other scientists. The system is driven by competition. The reputation system in science discourages real collaboration in an idea based system in favour of a politically driven personality based system.

Copyrights and patents are economic tools which frequently do not reward the idea originator and need to be replaced with something that does. Free information activists say information needs to be free and the originator can be rewarded by looking for other avenues of profit, such as public speaking. The idea that a scientist or other expert should waste their time traveling around appearing on panels and talk shows instead of following their passion and ability is illogical and counter-productive. By the time the general public has heard of a published work, most creative people have moved on to the next project, or would like to. If an expert wishes to speak, by all means, but if they do not they should still be able to work quietly and rely on the community to ensure they are credited and compensated. If celebrity is the path to recognition and financial reward then it is celebrity they will be seeking. Those spending time on actual research will have their ideas attributed to those building a following on Twitter and public speaking skills. Everyone has been conditioned to expect aggressive advertising from a creator, but better results could be obtained if the user group recognized product promotion as their responsibility and power.

Old corporate news media have nearly been humiliated out of their *Breaking! Exclusive! Scoop!* mentality with the news as they face a social media swarm that gets everything long before, or at least, at the exact same time that they do. The same change needs to happen with innovation and research, where those who hoard research lose to those who drop their ideas instantly and ask for crowd help. Reputation needs to come from visible open collaboration between scientists instead of secrecy and copyrighted publications. It is the responsibility of the user group, if they want innovators to concentrate on innovation and creators to concentrate on creating, to ensure that credit goes to the person researching, not necessarily the person seeking interviews. Research funding needs to be allocated in support of actions and ideas, and available to whoever accomplishes each task. In that way scientists can work on what they please without spending a huge amount of their time building up their personal brands and begging for funding.

Heather Marsh

Out of Robert Filmer's frying pan, into John Locke's fire

Chapter 36

The inequities in property ownership and governance today may be traced to a reaction to a form of governance espoused in Robert Filmer's *Patriarcha* which was used to justify the divine right of aristocracies. The complete absence of logic in Robert Filmer's insistence that "every man that is born is so far from being free, that by his very birth he becomes a subject of him that begets him" is nowhere dismantled more thoroughly than in John Locke's Two Treatises of Government. Locke then replaced Patriarchal dictates with an even more disastrous view of his own.

Two Treatises of Government is a strange medley of logic pieced together on selective authority from the Christian Bible, a very flawed understanding of zoology and a state of nature which has never existed for homo sapiens. Unfortunately for Locke's libertarian arguments, man has never been *"a lion or a tyger"* and may better look to bees and ants as models for behaviour. Locke's state of nature with unbridled free will has never existed except in isolated instances, as humans are social and do not act independently. He confused autonomy for all with an excess of free will, creating a survival of the fittest structure which allows autonomy only for a very few of the most ruthless.

Locke's happy assurance that a survival of the fittest structure would naturally result in a society *"wherein all the power and jurisdiction is reciprocal, no one having more than another"* and that *"Every man hath a right to punish the offender and be executioner of the law of nature"* but this will not occur *"according to the passionate heats, or boundless extravagancy of his own will"* would be entertaining if we were not all living in a world structured to his dictates. His insistence on a state of nature as not a reference point to improve but the ultimate goal is also curious. To say that what has always been is what always must be denies all of civilization.

The inconsistencies which claim inheritance as a right in a system following a labor theory of ownership and the naiveté throughout did not diminish the popularity of Locke's writing. Locke's influence was widespread and culminated in the most bald faced untruth to ever appear in a manifesto, Thomas Jefferson's assertion in the United States Declaration of Independence that *"all men are created equal"*, later repeated in France and elsewhere. The irony of a slave owner writing this did not stop this flawed principle from being used to construct a system of libertarianism that denied natural dependencies and relegated them to the fringes of society. There they were held to be aberrations caused by the dependents' own contrariness. This decentralized patriarchy no longer required noblesse oblige. Locke's libertarianism operated with a blithe disregard for what in a Patriarchal system would be obligations towards subjects who had to be cared for as one would children.

It does occur to Locke that women still do not come out quite as equal as others under his system. He contents himself with the reflection that they could do like Queens and just not marry, presumably if they were wise enough to have been born princesses. He argues that his patriarchy differs from Filmer's because his allows no power of life or death, therefore it cannot be slavery. This is in direct contradiction to the definition of freedom he requires for a free man who is at liberty to kill any who even takes one of his possessions. Theft of his property is an attempt to enslave a free man, rule over every aspect of a woman or child's life short of death is not. Other inequalities do not appear to occur to him, or are equated with greater virtue in the more powerful.

Locke's writings are the foundation for the system of dissociation we live in today. Societal pressure to respect and assist the needs of others was replaced by blame for the weak.

Charitable obligation was replaced by entitlement. Patriarchy was replaced by corporate power. Governance passed from families to cities to states to its first fully dehumanized form in corporations. The libertarian ideals assisted the powerful who considered it their free will to violate the rights of others in their quest for ever more power, the ultimate virtue in Locke's ideal state of nature.

Releasing chaos

Chapter 37

For those who read what I have written and think it is a fantastical utopian vision that can never be implemented, look again. Everything in this book exists and has always existed. Stigmergy is the natural path of collaboration that must be constantly regulated and fought with copyrights, patents, secrecy and ownership laws to be avoided. Personalities have been ignored throughout history as masses followed ideas which seemed beautiful and just. An approval economy is the natural economy we use every day and have since the first society. All societies are naturally systems of dependencies, not trade relationships. Epistemic communities have led our systems of knowledge since the first village elders. Each of us belongs to many rings of societies and user groups and each group has their own social contract. Individual rights are natural rights fought for by every mammal.

Why then does the world look so very different than anything in this book? It has taken violent coercive force, overwhelming propaganda and stripping the natural rights of individuals to a debilitating point to enforce the system we have today. There is nothing natural or easy about enforcing today's governance. Creators are forced to become destroyers, people are taught to seek goals that bring them no joy, the fulfillment of society has been lost to the bitterness of competition. A massive and ever-expanding system of military, security, surveillance and imprisonment is clamped on top of society worldwide to prevent any reversion to our natural methods. Our right to communicate is under constant attack as its power in swarm collaboration is increasingly recognized. The unending violence and destruction in the world today is caused by our natural reaction to these constrictions.

We now have the power to release the unnatural bindings that have us trapped in this horrible unnatural system of governance. We can walk across borders, refuse to participate in the financial system, refuse to recognize corporations, demand our human rights. We can build our own societies in the way that seems best to us and let the state powers implode. We have the power to leave.

Everything we need for a natural fulfilling society exists now, we only need to release it. If we refuse the bindings that have been placed on us, we will create a vacuum. If we allow that vacuum to be filled with the same system under a different name, we will be repeating the pattern of endless tyrannies we have repeated throughout history. To have governance by the people, we need to have faith in each other within chaos. A natural order or many natural orders can evolve and adapt and meet all of our challenges far more quickly than current repression and restraint. If we begin to look for and use the natural methods we already have and ignore the apparatus of dissociation, the former will grow and the latter will become obsolete. Chaotic methods do work to create social infrastructure, if we are aware of what we are trying to build. It is certain that not all solutions we create will be good. We have the power to reject those that are not.

Afterword

Afterword

In 2023, it feels like a lifetime ago that I wrote *Binding Chaos*. It's been interesting, reliving some of my thoughts from back then and remembering what inspired them.

At the time I was writing *Binding Chaos,* from 2010 until 2012, I was the sole editor and administrator of the Wikileaks news site.[56] At this time, Wikileaks and the major international news outlets were releasing US state cables that exposed corruption in governments around the world. This was not the everyday occurrence such massive leaks appear to be now - at the time, the public attention on the releases was extremely high. I tied the cables to current news stories and other information and amplified protests that resulted from the releases, as well as other corruption and oppression.[57] I left Wikileaks due to political, moral and journalistic differences on March 8, 2012. I was very grateful, however, that the massive megaphone I had in those years allowed me a platform and an incredible opportunity to amplify people fighting for human rights at a pivotal moment in history.

A primary goal of my work was expanding the public focus on men with guns to include women and children and people building communities. As I explain further in *The Creation of Me, Them and Us*, human rights topics were all but invisible in the news at that point, as were women and children. Even with that platform, it was very difficult to get these stories heard, but I discovered the power of using the image of a famous man to amplify stories that the public otherwise refused to listen to. I used my platform to launch and amplify many or most of the human rights movements that became known as the 2011 movements, including the Occupy movement.[58] A lot of the movements I was working with then were a product of austerity measures or other economic hardship, many were triggered by exposure of corruption in governments, and many were part of a contagion caused by the new ability to organize online.

The world of rapid, online debate was still very new. Even within protest movements, the most visible protesters were still from a small, elite group, and it was largely their concerns that were highlighted. I was invited to the 7th Berlin Biennialle in 2012, the only non-European who was flown there to be part of the exhibition of *"art that is smart and creative enough to take part in transformative social processes"*. [59] We used the modern art event as an opportunity for a months-long international assembly to discuss alternate methods of governance and more. When I walked into the kitchen of the space we were given, participants had covered the walls with inspirational quotes by famous people in many different handwritings. Every single one of the people quoted were men. (There were quotes by women elsewhere, but extremely few.) This was the world that those in the 2011 movements were from, but a few of them were ready for change.

The popular reforms at that time were centred around ideas like debt jubilees, cryptocurrencies and peer to peer trade. I spent long hours in international assemblies, trying to get people to understand that not everybody could borrow money or had anything to trade. Money was an extreme focus of protests in 2011 and earlier, as is reflected in a lot of *Binding Chaos*. I gave a keynote at the Alternate G8 summit in the UK in 2013[60] and talked about the ideas in *Binding Chaos*. The financial situation is not significantly changed today, but many women are now walking away from unpaid caregiving labour, whether that is through the trend to divorce among seniors or the refusal to have children or get married. Not only is domestic labour more recognized, emotional labour has also become a recognized term.

Now that women are no longer silently doing it all for free, the state of elder care is a crisis that is just beginning to be heard. This fight is just beginning to manifest. The economy is discussed in much more detail in a later book in this series, *The Power Economy*.

A primary feature of the 2011 movements was their attempt to avoid figureheads and hierarchy of the kind I was struggling with in Wikileaks and elsewhere. Unfortunately, this manifested largely in demands that everyone work selflessly and anonymously until the media could promote a figurehead to take credit for everyone else's work. There is a lot written in *Binding Chaos* about credit theft, due to the frequency with which this happened, especially when the movements finally reached the United States. Many of us had been organizing the US movement for months and years. In March 14, 2011, I announced the US movement on Wikileaks Central. That summer, many of us organized on mailing lists and Mumble and other chat forums for an international anti-banks day in the fall. By the time the protests finally arrived, on September 17, 2011, there was a lineup of figureheads waiting to claim credit for the movement, none of whom had been at all involved in its creation. This repeated again and again; people claimed credit because they were the first to use a hashtag, the first to announce on Twitter or the first to be promoted by US media when ideas were not coming from any of those places. Credit unclaimed does not disperse; it will be used to grant legitimacy to a figurehead. Once an idea had been identified with a figurehead, it was much easier to discredit and derail.

I retreated from exhausting assemblies and demands that everybody do the same work, and constantly communicate and reach consensus on their work, inspired to write about the need for epistemic communities and design communication tools that would be more useful at filtering signal from noise. I represented the Berlin Biennale hackathon at the World Free Media forum in Rio de Janeiro in June of 2012. A lot of my thinking about trust networks and reputation in *Binding Chaos* came from developing a prototype for Getgee, a project first initiated as the Global Square. I had spent a lot of time in the previous years, thinking about the problems inherent in web-based platforms and social media sealed wells. I appeared on BBC and in many free software forums and other venues over the next years, promoting an alternative.[61] This will be described in a later book in the *Binding Chaos* series, called *Code Will Rule*. The project went viral in international media when I initially proposed it, but in the end, it received no concrete support and was derailed by my growing list of opponents.

A significant number of these came from a part of the Internet underbelly called the chan boards. These forums, particularly 4chan and 8chan, were considered by many participants to be an anarchist utopia. In reality, both sites were dominated by predators who had been pushing their propaganda on young men and boys since the pre-Internet days of bulletin boards. These men had used the Internet and every earlier technology to communicate and share criminal media in secret. They made it their business to learn what they could about online security and used that knowledge to pose as hackers and impress young boys. Since the reason they required elite security was to share child rape media, the virulent propaganda they bullied and coerced young boys into accepting was the dehumanization of women and girls and the normalization of child rape as 'freedom of speech'. On the chan boards, because the majority of users posted anonymously, they began to call each other Anonymous.

The child rape advocacy group were on the chan boards in a battle for the hearts and minds of the next generation of men. Through the popularity of Wikileaks, I was able to intercept their influence and turn a large segment of their young targets to the other side. When supporters all over the world came out to defend Wikileaks and Julian Assange, I asked them to use the Anonymous banner which had recently entered mainstream news. In that way, I had a large number of connections globally who were both newly associated with Anonymous and supporters of

Wikileaks, and subsequently, my campaigns.

The predators who influenced the original Anonymous did not know what to do. They loved the new media popularity my campaigns brought them, but they hated me and their loss of influence over their young audience. At first, I started campaigns involving Wikileaks and political targets. No one else involved had my journalist background or my international networks to launch such a wide and diverse amount of campaigns, and neither did they want to. While they made edgy posts on Twitter, I was creating trends that they had to follow to seem relevant. Their accounts became huge, but they were forced to amplify my content. Once I had rebranded what Anonymous was, I moved to campaigns they hated even more.

An interesting thing about the predators who called themselves 'old Anonymous' is that the majority of them were being controlled by the spy agencies of the world, or anyone else who chose to threaten them, since they were so easily blackmailed by their criminal child predator activity. It was not surprising that they hated my campaigns against powerful people. They far preferred to mob children with hate campaigns. They were also often racist and hated campaigns that didn't centre the United States, or at least Europe. They tried to block my support of 2010 Tunisian protesters, which I pushed through by saying the activists had cable releases, so it was related to Wikileaks. After that, I simply launched campaigns using Tunisia as precedent.

A lot of the writing in *Binding Chaos* is related to campaigns I was working on at the time. Anonymous was one of several places I was field testing stigmergy as an organizational tool to counter my assembly exhaustion and figurehead frustration. I was growing a network of activists and developing a methodology, but I was also teaching an audience to look outside their customary Overton window. In opRohingya, I showed the world that the media was ignoring a genocide in Burma. In opGabon, I showed evidence that ritual killings were real and involved complicit politicians. In opCanary, I exposed criminal resource corporations and in Spooky Connections, I traced networks of powerful criminals and politicians. The public reaction and resistance to these campaigns is reflected in a lot of the ideas published later in *The Creation of Me, Them and Us.*

Many social media accounts that had gained huge followings on my previous campaigns tried to ignore these ones, but by then, I could use my large network and game the social media algorithms (and corporate media) to create trending topics on my own. My enemies threatened and blustered, and did anything they could to discredit me, but they were still benefitting from my campaigns and increasingly, those who picked up the Anonymous banner did so to join my campaigns. For several years, people insisted I ran a large bot network because everything I posted was instantly copied and reposted by dozens of other accounts who all sounded like me. I didn't run any other accounts. They just all picked up my content and repeated my principles. Still, my opponents used this story to pretend I was responsible for every bad thing that anybody said on the Internet for well over a decade.

Worse was yet to come for them when I used the movement formerly dominated by child rape advocates to advocate for child rape victims. *"An expanded network would also provide an avenue of appeal if a person felt their local society was shunning them unjustly or they were having their basic human rights violated."* This sentence was added during the Justice4Daisy / opMaryville campaign, covered in the Netflix documentary *Audrie & Daisy*.[62] This was one campaign of several that defended young girls like the ones the predators used to love to torment online. Daisy Coleman kept in touch for years afterwards and became a prominent human rights activist herself, amplified by the new version of Anonymous.

This began an era of many campaigns against rape and against rape advocates. Eventually, I launched opDeathEaters, a campaign which was written about in the 2016 book, *Crime, Justice and Social Media*[63] and featured in the 2022 Netflix documentary, *The Most Hated Man on the Internet.*[64] This went openly and directly against the predators that exerted so much influence on the chan boards, and their handlers. If we weren't at war before, we certainly were after 2014. Much has happened since *Binding Chaos* was written, and we will continue some of that story in *Free Will and Seductive Coercion.*

Those years were an adventure. I am the only person who was an early and influential part of all three of the most prominent movements of the last decade: Wikileaks, Occupy and Anonymous. One went down with a figurehead, one was crippled by consensus, and one was sabotaged by anonymity. These, and all the other movements I launched or amplified, were an incredible opportunity to conduct intensive research into methods of organization, coercion and power, while fighting for an end to oppression. It was exciting and a lot of work, but it became apparent long ago that a different approach is now required: slower, less exciting, but much more thorough. Hopefully, the series that I have been working on since *Binding Chaos* will be of some use in the coming era.

Heather Marsh

.

Glossary

Glossary

The following is a glossary of what I personally mean when I say these words. This is not an attempt to impose my definitions as the correct ones or an invitation to debate the definitions. It is only meant to apply to anything I say or write. As language is meant to be a shortcut to communication I try not to spend too much time discussing definitions. These books use definitions from universal reality unless otherwise noted. Terms using endoreality definitions are often denoted by single quotes.

Abstracting divinity:

1. The ways in which conscious and will have been disguised, hidden, denied and abstracted into ideas and institutions of governance, religion and science.

2. The methods through which the living access universal conscious and will, through anima banks, ritual and divination.

Alienation:

1. The process by which many smaller endogroups are created within a wider endogroup. This can happen organically as a wider endogroup dissolves or weakens, and it is also a political strategy used to weaken rival endogroups.

2. A separation created between two or more endogroups.

3. The separation of a part of the self, such as seen in those with refracted or amputated cores.

Alive:

1. An endoreality term for objects which meet an arbitrary threshold of animation and have not been authoritatively declared dead.

2. In Binding Chaos theory, the ability to access either primary or secondary anima is considered the defining feature of living.

Altruism: An exosocial act of assistance to another in order to create egalitarian balance.

America: Two continents and 35 countries.

American: Residents of any part of America.

Amputated core: The alienated part of a self caused when a person's own core is seen by them as an enemy outsider.

Anarchy: Society free of subordination to endogroups at any level. An exosocial society.

Androtheism: worship of men or gods in the form of men.

Anger: Anger can be defensive, dominant or predatory. Defensive anger is against external threat and can be experienced by anyone. Dominant anger is used to sublate another. Predatory anger is used to obtain secondary anima through the stress response of another.

Anglo / Germanic: Relating to states that speak primarily English and heavily adopt Anglo culture or are part of Germanic-speaking Europe. Notable for an industrial-scientific endo-idealism that took early precedence over the various church, filial or other endo-idealisms elsewhere. Recently, this group became the global endo-ideal through transcendental industrial-scientific endo-idealism. This is currently being replaced by the mono-empire.

Anima: life energy

Anima bank: A repository which contains surplus anima, obtained through sacrifice, devotion, offerings or interactions. An anima bank can be a person, dead or living, a rite, an object or an idea.

Anima conduit: A means of allowing the transfer of anima from a primary source.

Anima credit: A balance owed in a relationship or interaction where the subject has given more than they have received.

Anima debit: A balance owed in a relationship or interaction where the subject has received more than they have given.

Animus: Life energy contained within a personal or shared membrane for use by an individual or group.

Anima bloat: The overfilling of an animus with life energy.

Anonymous: A specific stigmergic method of collaboration and the people who use it.

Anxiety: An emotional response caused by fear of deanimation, meant to prevent exposure to potentially deanimating events.

Approval theory of value: The value of goods is based on the amount of social approval they represent.

Approval economy: Economy based on societal approval and acceptance.

Art: Creation which channels primary anima or acts as a capacitor for primary anima.

Asceticism: Depletion of energy in a personal animus by the will associated with the animus. asceticism under control of an external will is torture. There are three forms of asceticism: debt, Tantalus and punitive asceticism.

Authoritative endogroup: The endogroup with the coercive force available to enable them to define reality, morality, norms and law.

Auto-anima: Anima produced by feeding on oneself through asceticism, drugs or other attacks on one's own animus.

Auto-objects: People objectified by themselves who thereby become subjects with the power to objectify others.

Autocoercion: Transparent, consensual coercion a society applies onto itself.

Autogenocide: Genocide instigated remotely, usually though media incited sectarianism or trade of drugs or weapons to the targeted population, but performed by the population on itself.

Autohomicide:

1. Homicide instigated remotely, usually through violation and sublation techniques which destroy a personal membrane and leave the prey vulnerable to coercion by external wills.

2. Giving a negative image the desperation and means by which to destroy themselves, usually through self abuse, risk taking or suicide.

Autonomy:

1. Freedom from involuntary, unbalanced interactions aided by possession of a healthy personal membrane and a network of primary anima sources and conduits.

2. Governance by user group including governance of self for those things which impact only self.

Billion: A billion is a million million (bi + million), but the US. changed it to mean a thousand million so that they could have 'billionaires'. The two definitions are now known as the short scale and long scale definitions. This is a classic example of reality manipulation to serve an exceptional myth and endo-identity created from magical words subject to the whim of the endo-ideal.

Binding Chaos:

1. The natural method of using extrapolation, experience and experimentation to bind chaotic input into ordered packets of information as our brains are designed to do.

2. The use of extreme coercive force to prevent chaotic

systems from living, evolving or creating change.

3. The transition from primordial chaos to a world of ordered objects.

4. Endosocialism.

Black box words: Words with no definition other than circular, often used to pretend a meaning where none is known or disguise a meaning which is against the authoritative endoreality. Examples are *nothing,* imagination, and *random.* In the *Binding Chaos* series, black box words are used when the full definition is unknown. An example is *anima conduit.*

Body: A physical form, one of the five elements of a person.

Boredom: A sign of severe distress which occurs when someone is offered an interaction which they cannot access or a third party is attempting to intercept an interaction or there is no interaction available. Boredom is the inability or refusal to exercise will and seek interaction. This is the chronic condition of an endoself.

Bureaucrats: People with institutional authority to exert their will over the interactions of others.

Butterfly: An idea which can cause a hurricane of change. Reference to the butterfly effect.

Capacitor: A cluster of interactions in the form of an object, rite or idea which serves as an anima bank. A capacitor stores an excess of anima which can be accessed in other times and places.

Caregiver: A person whose work involves the care of other people, animals, communities or ecosystems.

Caregiver-self: A circle of expansion which includes or replicates those relationships first formed by a baby or small child with their home and caregivers, particularly if that circle has created an endogroup.

Centripetal force: A force which acts on unequal populations in forced interactions to create ponzi schemes of celebrity, wealth and power and endogroups. Slight advantages become huge by the requirement that everyone support those with resources or power in order to benefit. This force creates and upholds endogroups and is an endosocial force.

Centrifugal force: An egalitarian force which acts in opposition to ponzi schemes and endogroups. This force serves to either strengthen the existing ponzi scheme by increasing the defending force or collapse it. This is an exosocial force.

Censorship by noise: Using celebrity or official status to amplify certain voices or opinions to the disadvantage of others who may have better or opposing information. Using astroturfing spam for the same purpose.

Channeler: A person with the ability to channel prolific amounts of primary anima, often through art, which differs from craft due to this added feature.

Charity: An endosocial act of giving which results in establishing the giver as the endo-ideal and the receiver as the negative image. This differs from altruism in the fact that no connection is established and debt and guilt are incurred by the receiver, along with a negative image status.

Circle of self / circle of expansion: Clusters of relationships and interactions that form naturally or through coercion as a person's self develops from birth onward. These clusters may form into endogroups and block further expansion. They often occur at the levels of lifegiver, caregiver, nation, discovery, creation or divinity.

Civilization: A vast network of interception points for sublation of interactions and interception of anima.

Class: A social construct (endoreality) resulting from classification of people relative to the endo-ideal. Modern usage is usually related to wealth endo-idealism.

Cognitive dissonance: Distress caused by a conflict between dominant and authoritative endoreality, between universal reality and endoreality or between an endoreality believed in the past and what the subject believes now.

Colonization: sublation of the will and animus of a nation.

Commoner: A stable majority created to uphold the status quo, or overthrow it during times of revolution. Societal structures are designed for the comfort and coercion of commoners. Mass acceptance of this role creates a solid block of uniform opinions which can be used to create and uphold oligarchy and ostracize witches and wretches. Reflector at a state level or higher.

Community: A group affiliated around allocation of common resources. Communities may be societies, where allocation is through social relationships, or trade economies, where allocation is through trade.

Concentric circle: Peer promoted voices or ideas in a transparent, permeable structure where those at the centre receive the most amplification and ideas are audited and taught to the outer circles by knowledge bridges.

Connection:

1. A balanced interaction.

2. An anima conduit constructed with balanced interactions.

Connection nihilism: The idea that all connections are qualitatively the same and there is no added value to bonded people, objects, ritual or ideas. A denial of the existence of euphoric objects.

Conscious: All that exists. Awareness of every interaction that makes up universal reality, from all perspectives. Universal knowledge.

Conscious will: A will controlled by the conscious. Conscious will chooses the path of greater entropy through dispersal of personal energy, usually in the creation of order.

Consciousness: Filtered, condensed, modified and individuated awareness of a part of conscious, presented from the perspective of a specific will's position in a self. This awareness is limited to only those interactions within zero degrees of the subject will and initiated through conscious control of will. This subset of reality is subjected to the laws of endoreality through an endofilter.

Contempt: Shame and guilt are punished by contempt, an emotion directed downwards from the endo-ideal to the reflectors or negative image and from the reflectors to the negative image to increase their separation from guilt.

Corporate feminism: Feminism which emanated from the United States in the 1960s and was heavily guided by both the CIA and corporate interests. It created an endogroup out of a global exosocial struggle for women's liberation.

Corporate masculinism: A political movement which began in the 1970s to advocate against women's liberation under the guise of men's rights. It is heavily guided by the primarily criminal sexual sublation and sexual violation industries as well as many state and religious bodies. The objective is to continue the enslavement of women for domestic labour, baby production and the rape industry. The objective is the oppression of women, but the target of coercion is men.

Crabs in a pot: If only one crab is placed in a pail, they can easily escape, but if more than one are there, they will each other back from any attempt to escape. This is used as a metaphor or simile for similar social behaviour.

Creation-self: A circle of expansion which includes those relationships related to creation. This is often trapped into a career endogroup.

Creation euphoria: The euphoria obtained from the act of creation. This can be stored in a euphoric object.

Credit: Anima owed to the prey of unbalanced interactions in order to achieve egalitarian balance.

Culture: The rites, objects and ideas that connect a national animus through space and time. This may include dances, songs, art, spirituality, some aspects of creation, rituals, and euphoric objects.

Currency:

1. Abstract, dissociated approval which allows access to all benefits of society without contribution, membership or acceptance of the society's values or norms.

2. Endosocial token to replace gratitude and approval and replace exosocial interactions with endosocial transactions.

3. A capacitor which contains anima in an easily exchanged format.

4. A talisman for transferring the guilt in an unbalanced interaction to the recipient.

Curse: Attribution of guilt through the assigning of a negative image status along with the guilt. Often used alongside punishment, i.e. screaming the curse while beating or killing someone assigns them the blame for their own victimhood.

Deanimation: the loss or depletion of life from an animus. Deanimation often results in physical manifestations such as low stress resistance, weakened immunity, adrenal exhaustion, depression or other weakness and can result in serious illness or death.

Dead: A state of low animation that occurs on a spectrum. An endoreality term used to authoritatively assign an attribute and define some objects and formerly living things as not living.

Death: The decoupling of the five elements of a person (body, self, life, will and consciousness) in such a way that they often cannot be rejoined.

Death Eaters: Members of a society where the norms or culture are driven by sadism. The agony of others is not a side effect of their actions but a goal. Death eaters are distinct from those with an individual personality disorder in that their society's norms, structure and actions are all constructed to feed their sadism.

Decoupled: a person whose five elements (body, self, life, will and consciousness) have been dissociated from each other and are no longer bound into a unified person.

Debt: Anima owed by a predator in unbalanced interactions in order to achieve egalitarian balance.

Debt asceticism: asceticism which causes joy through the release from debt and guilt brought by a lessening of anima bloat.

Democracy: Governance by representative or direct voting systems.

Demographics: Objectification and alienation of people through further division of the already objectified populations, usually in an attempt to create new endogroup identities for coercion.

Depression: A state of deanimation. This may be caused by blocked or ruptured conduits, unrequited interactions, an inhibited will, shame, sublation or violation.

Dignity: Preservation of ownership over one's own inner circles of self. This ownership creates personal integrity and strength.

Discovery-self: A circle of expansion which contains those relationships unique to discovery. This is often trapped into an academic endogroup.

Dissociation:

1. Separation of individuals from the dependency relationships which make up society.

2. Separation of self in the case of refracted or amputated cores.

3. Separation of conscious, self or will from each other.

Diversity: There is diversity between every two humans. In endoreality, this term is used to create endo-identities, which is the opposite of diversity. The concept could be replaced with anti-endo-idealism. A better path would be to simply point out endo-idealism and leave anti-endo-idealism as the default state.

Divinity: A loosely defined term representing sometimes the universal or quantum will and sometimes the conscious. This is possibly also Jung's *collective unconscious* and the source of Kant's *synthetic a priori knowledge*. In the *Binding Chaos* series it is used to refer to universal conscious and will as they are referenced colloquially.

Divinity-self: the self created by euphoric interactions with divinity. These can include spiritual sources but can also be found in everyday euphoric sources, whether or not the subject experiences them as spiritual. Any interaction with primary anima or the conscious expands the divinity self. The divinity self is often trapped into a religious endogroup.

Divination: The attempted acquisition of divine (universal conscious) knowledge or divine (universal will) choice through skill, following a methodology. Some rationalism and even some science falls under this category.

Dominant endogroup: The endogroup which has the subject person or population most immersed in its endoreality or most sublated to it.

Economy:

1. Resource allocation.

2. When referred to as *the economy*, it serves as an anima bank or god for wealth endo-idealism.

Emotion: Response to anticipation or experience of access to anima or anticipation or experience of an attack on an anima source.

Emotional will: A will controlled by the self and motivated solely by potential anima gain or loss.

Empathic bond: An empathic conduit that is strong and somewhat permanent.

Empathic conduit: The means by which understanding can be shared or jointly experienced between two sources.

Empathy: The ability to share understanding with another through empathic conduits.

Endo-exceptionalism: Adherence to the exceptional myth of an endogroup.

Endo-ideal: The idealized self of an endogroup, embodying all virtue, ownership, victimhood and credit.

Endo-ideal sublation: Sublation of will to an endo-ideal.

Endo-idealism: Adherence to the laws of endoreality which attribute all virtue, ownership, victimhood and credit to the endo-ideal and all vice, guilt and punishment to the negative image.

Endo-identity: A magical word used to set an endogroup off as exceptional and create difference where none exists.

Endofilter: A cognitive filter which causes the subject to filter all information from universal reality according to the laws of endoreality. This includes the endoreality experienced by humans as macroscopic objects and the perception commonly accepted as 'sane'.

Endogroup: A social structure for creating power through the transfer of energy. A group of affiliated people who use inclusion and shunning to define their society and are bound by an endosocial membrane. An endogroup may be temporally unlimited to allow ownership and appropriation of property, culture, achievements and victimhood from generations past. An endogroup includes six components:

- An identity which enables exclusive membership. May be referred to as an endo-identity or a [specific endogroup] identity, ie state identity, race identity, etc.

- An idealized source of collective reality, residing in a person or ideology. May be referred to as an endo or exo-ideal or a [specific endogroup] ideal, ie scientific-industrial ideal, religious ideal, etc.

- An existential threat from external forces.

- An exceptional myth justifying unequal entitlement. May be referred to as an exceptional myth or a [specific endogroup] myth, ie nation myth, family myth, etc.

- A negative image, made up of people identified as opposite the ideal. May be referred to as a negative image or a [specific endogroup] negative image, ie wealth negative image, health negative image, etc.

- Reflectors which may exist separately from the negative image in groups of more than two. May be referred to as a reflector or a [specific endogroup] reflector, ie academic reflector, male reflector, etc.

Endogroup sublation: Sublation of will to an endogroup.

Endoreality: A reality which exists only within an endogroup and is created with the laws of endoreality. Endoreality is filled with magical words which have no universal meaning but serve to cast people as the negative image or endo-ideal. Endoreality is relative and has no meaning outside the perspective of the endogroup. Endoreality can change at the whim of an endo-ideal.

Endoself: A predator who can only exist, or prefers to exist, through acquisition of secondary anima.

Endoself contagion: The process by which exosocial interactions are blocked and discouraged in a population of endoselves, leading exosocial people to develop endoself behaviours through necessity.

Endosocial: Existing within the confines of an endogroup or endoself or according to the laws of endoreality.

Endosocial membrane: A membrane which blocks empathic and euphoric conduits and thereby creates endoselves and endogroups.

Endosocial martyrdom: Anima is forcibly taken from the idol and distributed to the masses.

Endosocial tyranny: Anima is forcibly taken from the masses and distributed to the endo-ideal.

Endosocialism: The belief that societies ought to be ordered within endogroup power structures.

Envy: The sense of injustice felt by members of an endogroup if external acclaim or a coveted item is held by someone outside the endogroup or its endo-ideal.

Epistemic community: A way to provide elite expertise for projects without relinquishing control to an elite oligarchy. People or ideas are peer promoted from within the user group and communities remain transparent and permeable to everyone.

Acceptance or rejection of ideas is always up to the user group to avoid an unassailable oligarchy. Typically organized in transparent, permeable concentric circles.

Equality: An observably false idea that all people are equal used to justify imposing involuntary interactions of unequal force on diverse populations. This results in power accumulation and endosocialism.

Equivalence: The idea that all members of a society are entitled to equivalent benefit from the society and no one should be valued by standards of achievement which others have greater ability to attain. No contribution to society is inherently of greater value than another although the degree of effort may be. This is an idea which supports exosocialism.

Escapism: Entertainment which provides easy secondary anima and does not challenge endoreality. Escapism strengthens the emotional will over the conscious will. It is easier to watch because it does not require an expenditure of energy through the focus of the conscious will.

Euphoria: The emotional experience of anima, or life energy.

Euphoric bond: A euphoric conduit that is strong and somewhat permanent.

Euphoric conduit: A path or method allowing the transfer of anima from one source to another. An anima conduit.

Euphoric depletion: Deanimation.

Euphoric interaction: one which results in a net gain in primary anima.

Euphoric object: An object which contains anima from its creator or previous or current owners and can be used as a capacitor to connect an extended self through space and time.

Exceptional lives: Lives which are given far more value by media and society due to endo-ideal status.

Exceptional myth: Exceptional myths encourage both unjustified glorification of the group and its endo-ideal and unjustified demonization of the negative image as well as other endogroups and their endo-ideals. The five primary types of exceptional myths address creation, leaders, superiority, persecution and destiny. A purely magical creation, like the endo-identity; its purpose is its function, not its meaning.

Excitement: The anticipation of primary or secondary anima.

Exo-ideal: The idealized centre of an endogroup where the primary energy transfer flows from the idol to the rest of the group.

Exogroup: This does not exist as an exogroup is simply a cluster of interactions.

Exoself: A person with no, or very few, endosocial attachments and a large exosocial network.

Exosocial: Pertaining to exosocial expansion.

Exosocial expansion: Uninhibited expansion of self by continual establishment of euphoric conduits through relationships, discovery, creation, spirituality, etc to primary anima sources.

Exosocial networks: Created by conduits between primary sources of anima to allow balanced euphoric interactions.

Exosocialism: The belief in universal freedom to uninhibited exosocial expansion.

Extranational: Existing outside national or state structures.

Extroversion: Enjoyment of social interactions as a source of anima.

Face: An integral part of a person, signifying a healthy personal membrane, free of debt or unreleased credit and able to establish balanced connections.

Fear: Fear is anticipation of an attack on a anima source. In a primarily exosocial person, the feared attack is on an anima conduit or source. In a primarily endosocial person, the feared attack is on an endogroup or endo-ideal.

Feminism: The belief in the liberation of women to fulfill their full potential through uninhibited exosocial expansion. The word feminism is a poor substitute for the concept of women's liberation. Removal of male and other types of endo-idealism would be much more helpful in achieving liberation than establishment of endogroup feminism.

Festival: An event for producing a surge of primary and/or secondary anima from a variety of sources. Festivals are common before life threatening events such as war or winter and in the creation of shared animus such as marriage or coronations,

First age of nations: A great variety of autonomous and complete societies, occasionally networked and sharing or trading with each other, which people lived in for hundreds of thousands of years.

Forbidden chamber: A construction which conceals and forbids access to secrets of the guilt of the powerful. This supports the endoreality law that knowledge of endo-ideal guilt is a greater offence than any crime committed by the endo-ideal. See also Secret chamber guilt.

Fourth age of nations: A potential society we could develop, more diverse, flexible and mutually supportive than the first tribal one and more rewarding and universally beneficial than the third parasitical, supranational one.

Fraternity: Decentralized patriarchy resulting from politics which espoused Liberty, Equality, Fraternity. Fraternity as a goal is not suitable to global collaboration as it implies both equality and unanimity of principles. It has resulted in a fraternity of endo-ideals aligned under endosocialism. They still claim the right to control the lives of other people and occupy the top strata of society, like patriarchy, but now they bear no responsibility for governance or any participation in society.

Gaslighting: Assertion of the laws of endoreality through denial of universal reality and guilt reversal.

Gender: A social construct (endoreality) created in order to impose power relations based on sex with a male endo-ideal and a female negative image.

Genocide: The murder of a nation.

Ghosts: Decoupled but undispersed animus. These may be interaction clusters with an imbalance, either credit or debit.

Gift: Goods or services allocated to a person who is not automatically entitled to a share by social norms, or goods or services one is not automatically entitled to by social norms, such as personal or rare property. Gifts are not an entitlement and frequently carry expectations such as eventual reciprocity or future friendship.

God: An anima bank with a will which allocates life energy according to whim, supplication, deception or justice.

Governance:

1. Endosocial definition: Enforced subordination to an endo-ideal and enforced membership in an endogroup.

2. Exosocial definition: Caretaker responsibility of the user group.

Gratitude: A feeling of good will and admiration directed towards the provider in an altruistic interaction.

Guilt: The debt from an unbalanced interaction. Guilt is transferable.

Gynophobia: Terror of women, the fear of becoming or being cast as a woman (the negative image), or fear of the loss of patriarchal power or male endo-idealism. Gynophobia is particularly prevalent in those with an amputated core.

Gynotheism: worship of women or gods in the female form.

Hate: The experience of the expenditure of energy in creating or defending an endosocial membrane.

Holosocial: A social group which includes everyone. May be exosocial but may also refer to endosocialism under a global mono-empire.

Homo economicus: The endo-ideal of classical economists. A pure endoself, with no goals outside of the exploitation of others for accumulation of personal power.

Honour: Hierarchical approval awarded from the endo-ideal, signifying the state of not being the negative image.

Hope: Conscious striving for exosocial connection or relief from sublation or violation. To lose hope is to stop seeking connection or liberation.

Hostile seductive coercion: An external force of seductive coercion with interests in opposition to the subject.

Idea based collaboration: Collaboration that develops or verifies an idea or information.

Idol: The idealized self or anima bank for an endogroup.

Ideologues: Members of endogroups with an exceptional myth based on ideas attributed to them or ideas they adhere to.

Independence: The state of living free from dependencies. This is impossible in reality but can be simulated by the use of currency to abstract dependency and endosocialism to deny the labour of the negative image.

Imagination: A black box word used to describe glimpses of conscious outside of personal perspective. This often appears in dreams or a trance state.

Incel: An acolyte of an offshoot of corporate masculinism which uses the dehumanization and debasement of women to manipulate men. The associated propaganda encourages men to be anti-social and suicidal, and incites acts of domestic terrorism. It appears to be heavily influenced by rival state agencies.

Indigenous: Customs or hereditary members of a community which follows a first or second age culture of the subject region.

Infidelity: Embezzlement of the energy of a shared animus to feed outside interactions or an external animus, particularly in monogamous, romantic relationships.

Inhumanity: A lack of empathy and denial of the need of others to live dignified lives.

Integrity: Strength of personal membrane and exosocial network.

Interaction: An action involving two entities, initiated by will, using energy from life, occurring in one spacetime. Irreversible units of conscious. The base unit of the universe. Interactions are clustered into individual selves by endosocial membranes which exist only in endoreality. Interactions may be balanced, rebuffed, unrequited or predatory resulting in events and relationships of connection, sublation or violation.

Interaction self: The true self, composed of networks of interactions.

Introversion: Fear of social interaction because of experienced deanimation.

Inverted debt: Guilt or debt which is transferred to a benefactor so that the beneficiary feels ever-increasing credit or entitlement instead of gratitude or guilt.

Iron law of oligarchy: Theory of Robert Michels, *"Who says organization, says oligarchy"*. This theory says that oligarchy is inevitable and it is used as a justification for fascism. Oligarchy is inevitable under endosocialism but not through exosocialism.

Jealousy: Fear of a negative change to one's own endogroup status due to the relative rise of another.

Joy: The experience of euphoria caused by available and secure connections to primary anima. An endoself may feel excitement, but never joy.

Kindness: Collective term describing the actions which offer shared anima to others.

Knowledge bridge: People who help disseminate information from an expert to a novice level of understanding and collectively audit what the epistemic community is doing. Besides being essential for education and auditing, this is important to avoid demagogues who have the ability and time to develop mass appeal but are not the source of expertise. Epistemic communities and knowledge bridges allow elite expertise a direct path of communication to the entire user group and provide a path for anyone in the user group to promote ideas and achieve elite expertise if they wish.

Laughter: A method of sharing euphoria and a reaction to the experience of euphoria or awareness of endoreality. The seven types of laughter are experience of euphoria, self affirmation, self destruction, social affirmation, social exclusion, endogroup domination and endogroup submission.

Laws: Coercive strictures which reflect the laws of endoreality for the authoritative endogroup.

Liberation: Freedom to continue exosocial expansion.

Libertarian: Desirous of liberty, as the freedom to do anything one desires, without social responsibility or acknowledgment of debt. This is a very popular ideology among endoselves.

Liberty: Coercion, responsibility and dependency are part of all human existence. The endosocial illusion of liberty for a few is created through dissociation, enabled by the trade economy. Exosocial liberty is freedom from involuntary interactions of unequal force (sublation and violation) and freedom to continue exosocial expansion through connection.

Life: The energy which is used to create interactions. Life force expands outward through interactions with other sources of life energy. Exosocial expansion can be blocked or deviated through the use of a greater opposing force.

Lifegiver: A woman who has given birth.

Lifegiver-self: The initial self created by the shared animus and cluster of interactions between a lifegiver and an infant.

Living:

1. An attraction to anima and a continual quest to assure its availability.

2. The exercise of will to create interactions.

Loneliness: A melancholy state of longing caused by unrequited connections or a lack of opportunity to establish connections.

Love: The flow of enetrgy through a connection to a primary anima source. Love has three stages: *attraction*, marked by excitement and intense curiosity, *connection*, marked by joy in sharing anima, and formation of a *shared animus*, at which point destruction of the new shared self would cause severe trauma. Love is created by the conscious will.

Lust: Avarice, or a desire for possession in order to obtain secondary anima. Lust has three stages, which are *lust*, manifesting as an intense desire for possession, *possession*, during which the endoself seeks complete ownership or sublation of the target and outside reflection in the form of admiration of their new possession and lastly, *disillusionment*, boredom and punishment of the object which is blamed for the disappointment. Lust emanates from the emotional will.

Magic: The deliberate use of skill and methodology to achieve any of the following:

1. Creation of endosocial barriers and endorealities.

2. Causing ideas or people to be shunned or accepted through the creation of endogroups, endo-ideals and negative images. Sublation of one will to another through creation of a shared animus or bond. Modern examples are employment contracts or student enrollment.

3. The transfer of energy, guilt and debt, especially through the use of magic words and ritual, including curses and protective spells. *Diplomatic immunity* is an example of a modern spell, complete with talismans, to ward off curses carrying guilt (criminal accusations).

4. Access of information from the universal conscious or guidance of choice or outcome from the universal will through divination.

5. Rituals around guilt allocation, guilt deflection and punishment are now largely under the jurisdiction of law and economy. Divination and influence of outcomes was first transferred to prayer and is now controlled by economics. Bondage and sublation is now the business of government.

Magic words: Words whose usage is unrelated to their meaning in universal reality. Words used solely for the purpose of magic, such as creating an endogroup or endoreality or casting information as authoritative or not based on association with the endo-ideal or negative image.

Martyr: The idol of an endogroup where anima flows from the idol to the rest of the group. An exo-ideal.

Masculinism: Male endo-idealism.

Masculinist theory: Theory based on research that only includes men or is presented from an exclusively male point of view or which sets the experience of men as the normative standard.

Megaphone: A platform able to reach a large number of people.

Migratory endo-ideals: When a transcendental endogroup has an overpopulated group of endo-ideals, or they are under pressure, they will begin to swarm by creating a multitude of smaller endogroups at lower levels. This results in alienated societies and in the colonization of negative image groups both within and without the original endogroup.

Mono-empire: The transcendental global empire at the end of the third age of nations. This is a transitional phase as a mono-empire has no outside opposition and can therefore never fully form.

Nation: Layered and overlapping societies gathered for community, cooperation and sharing, and existing across borders and generations. Nations may include sacred objects, rites, land and culture which facilitate connection across distances of time and space.

Nation-self: A circle of expansion which contains those relationships unique to a nation. This is often trapped into a state endogroup.

Negative image: An endogroup role which causes a person to adopt the perspective of an external endo-ideal and uphold the laws of endoreality. This role acts as the inverse of the endo-ideal. It embodies all vice, guilt and shame assignment within the endogroup.

Neo-necromancer: The powerful of the third age who seek to control populations through occupation of their most intimate circle of self, that containing control over the body, consciousness, self, will and life.

Nightmares: Perception of glimpses of unfiltered earthbound reality.

Nothing: A state that cannot exist. This is a black box word used by those who choose to deny the existence of whatever they are describing as nothing.

Object: an animus, an energy cluster held together by a dominant will, perceived as individuated.

Object self: A self with an endosocial membrane which is difficult to penetrate or create connections through. An endoself.

Outgroup: A population not included in, or shunned by, an endogroup. This does not include the negative image which is within the endogroup.

Paedosadist: There is no such thing as a sexual orientation called paedophilia. A sexual orientation, or sex, requires consenting partners. It is not sex if some of those involved are called victims, that is rape. Someone attracted to rape has sexual sadism disorder or paraphilic coercive disorder. Someone attracted to the rape of children is a paedosadist. A paedosadist who acts on their impulses is a criminal paedosadist and one who does not is a non-offending paedosadist. This definition is for those relying on the DSM as authority. A more appropriate term is the legal one, child rapist.

Parasite: Predator who obtains secondary anima by intercepting interactions between two primary sources, exhausting open anima conduits and leaving no reward for the initiator of interactions.

Passive genocide: The denial of life essentials to populations where people will die without access to them.

Patriarchy: A form of male and filial endo-idealism with a hierarchical social structure and a paternal elder as each family endo-ideal. Often inaccurately used to describe male endo-idealism.

Pedosadist: US spelling, see paedosadist definition.

Person: A temporarily bound unit containing a body, self, life, will and consciousness that appear as an individuated, cohesive whole.

Personality: A pattern of conscious and emotional responses to anima attraction and repulsion governed by conscious and emotional control over will.

Personal membrane: A strong and permeable boundary around the inner circle of self which controls intimacy and permits the establishment of euphoric and empathic conduits.

Philosophy: A framework for viewing and analyzing large, fundamental areas of knowledge and experience. A philosophy is based on foundational principles which work in diverse situations. Mechanism and animism are philosophies.

Philosopher: A person who has developed a complete, coherent, original body of fundamental ideas known as a philosophy.

Photoshop: Remove aspects of a story which the writer does not deem relevant or agree with and leave only those which support the writer's bias.

Ponzi scheme:

1. A pyramid scheme algorithm which requires those at the bottom to support those at the top in order to benefit. This type of scheme never benefits more than a few.

2. Social structure in which everyone tries to acquire celebrity, wealth and power, creating a centripetal force that holds oligarchs in place. Egalitarian systems imposed on unequal populations tend to ponzi.

Population: The people objectified and possessed by the endo-ideals of an endogroup.

Power:

1. The ability to control interactions through exertion of greater force. Power is based on energy acquired through unequal force in interactions. There is no idle or inert power and there is no benevolent power.

2. Social approval that causes others to identify with and emulate the powerful ahead of themselves or others. This power can be used to realize one's own will or include or shun the will or person of others and it can also be used to accumulate wealth, celebrity, credit or any other offering that the social group brings. Once this power is established, it provides the unequal force which can be used to turn every interaction into a transaction in which the powerful gain more power.

Power economy: An economy in which every interaction is a transaction, or an energy exchange in which no connections are established.

Predation: Obtaining secondary anima through involuntary interactions of unequal force. A predatory interaction drains energy from one agent, the prey, and that energy is picked up by the other agent, the predator.

Predator: One who obtains secondary anima from others through stress, pain, obstruction and destruction. The three types of predator are: Parasite, sublator and violator.

Prey: Those who lose secondary anima to others through stress, pain, obstruction and destruction. Those suffering damaged personal membranes and deanimation, or channelers of primary anima with no method of protecting themselves from predatory or egalitarian forces, are often prey. Prey either is or becomes the negative image.

Pride: An endo-ideal emotion. A surge of power and affirmation of their endo-ideal status.

Primary anima: Anima obtained through conscious connection to primary sources. Primary anima produces euphoria and prolongs life.

Primary euphoria: Euphoria obtained through conscious connection to primary anima sources.

Privacy: Privacy is ownership of an individual membrane, control over one's own circles of intimacy and the ability to establish one's own boundaries of intimacy. Privacy is sovereignty over the most intimate circle of self. It includes control over the body, thought and interactions.

Punitive asceticism: asceticism as a form of self-flagellation, debasement, deprivation or severe challenge in which the target extracts anima from their own stores (auto-anima) through punishment and shaming. They are then able to experience euphoria from the release of anima, just as predators experience euphoria when anima is released from their prey.

Quantum will: The chooser behind the choice of outcome in quantum interactions.

Race: A social construct (endoreality) created in order to impose power relations by arbitrary classifications. These have historically included sex, economic class, real or imagined heredity and colourism. The concept, or word, has been sometimes expanded recently (primarily in the United States) to include ideological belief, ancestral language, and self identification.

Random: This is a black box word used by those who choose to deny that every choice includes that which chooses, aka a will. It is usually used to describe an event decided by the quantum will. It is impossible to create a random event in code because random does not exist.

Reaction: A movement demanding change back to a time when a larger portion of the people at the top of the ponzi scheme of power benefitted from it. Reactionaries have no interest in changing underlying principles or helping those at the bottom except with promises of reforms trickling down. Reforms in a ponzi scheme will never trickle down as what feeds the top, bleeds the bottom.

Reanimation: The gain of life energy in an animus.

Ren: A Confucian term once translated as manliness, which is, in the old sense of the word man, humanity. Ren is described most clearly in *The Analects* where it mentions equitable relationships and healthy self-valuation. Ren may be somewhat equivalent to face or personal membrane.

Reflection: The process whereby the empathic conduits of a person are all directed to an external endo-ideal and they act as an obedient enforcer of the laws of endoreality.

Reflector: An endogroup role which causes a person to adopt the perspective of an external endo-ideal and uphold the laws of endoreality. A reflector is seen as obedient and selfless and so avoids the guilt and shame assignment of the negative image. They sublate their own will to the endo-ideal to avoid guilt.

Refraction: The process whereby a person's core self is redirected to an external self and they give up all autonomy and will to the occupying endo-ideal. Extreme dissociation can result from refraction.

Repeater: A rite or action which brings forth another cluster of interactions from a different spacetime.

Resistance: Building new systems and exosocial networks and defending them against oppressive coercion.

Revolution: A change of the top of a power structure, usually replacing an old oligarch with a representative of the largest or most powerful negative image group. The paradigm remains unchanged.

Revolutionary event: One in which an endo-ideal becomes the negative image for a portion of their former obedient reflectors.

Rites: A practice which can be used as a capacitor or repeater to connect an extended self through space and time.

Sandbox villages: Societies (which do not have to be geographically defined) for trying out new ideas for governance and collaboration.

Saviour: A person who replenishes the anima of others and reflects an idealized image of those they save. A reflector.

Science: Science: 1. A research methodology. 2. A set of ideologies and philosophies used as frameworks to interpret research data. 3. An endo-identity. 4. An endoreality term for an authoritative source of knowledge under scientific – industrial endo-idealism.

Scientific superstition: Fear by scientists of looking at topics outside of their endoreality which is largely the perspective of endo-ideals. Superstition causes a refusal to study, or even acknowledge, anything associated with their negative image, primarily women and indigenous people, or associated with rival endogroups, primarily religion.

Sealed well: Databases of public information which have access controlled by corporate owned web pages and apps.

Second age of nations: Hierarchical trade empires which included a powerful extranational merchant class.

Secondary anima: Anima obtained through fear or other stress responses of another, or destruction. It does not result in the experience of joy, improvement of health or the creation of primary anima conduits. It results in highs, crashes and cravings instead of the peace brought by secure primary anima conduits. It eventually helps to create an endoself which is no longer able to access primary anima.

Secondary euphoria: The experience of secondary anima obtained through sublation or violation.

Secrecy: Ownership and control over the intimate knowledge of another or involving another.

Secret chamber guilt: A tool of guilt reversal where the discovery of guilt is depicted as more grievous than the original act. Secret chamber guilt is used to negate original guilt and justify guilt, shame and punishment being passed to the accuser instead of the accused. It represents the law of endoreality which dictates that the endo-ideal may never be assigned guilt; therefore, the accuser is guilty of breaking the laws of endoreality by doing so. Under industrial or state endo-idealism, secret chamber guilt is often enforced by law. See also Forbidden chamber.

Seductive coercion: Seduction is coercion through emotional attraction and repulsion. Such coercion includes manipulation and control of information by authoritative endoreality. It is often based on shunning and inclusion.

Self: The unique positioning of an individual relative to others connected through a network of interactions.

Self-governance: Governance by user group.

Sex: There are three powers of sex. The exosocial power creates strong euphoric and empathic bonds and eventually, a shared animus with another person. The endosocial power creates an endosocial membrane, with the subjects joined within the membrane or divided by it. The endogroup power can be used to sublate one self to another within an endogroup membrane.

Sexual connection: Sexual interactions which establish connection.

Sexualized sublation: Interactions of humiliation or sublation promoted as sex to disguise their nature.

Sexualized violence: Violent interactions promoted as sex to disguise their nature.

Shame: Shame is the experience of deanimation caused by being assigned guilt and the internalization of the perception of the self as the negative image. Shame inhibits the establishment of euphoric conduits or connection.

Shame killing: The murder of a negative image to eradicate shame assigned to a sublated endo-ideal or endogroup by the transcendental endo-ideal or endogroup. Shame killings are often referred to by the euphemism *honour killings* when they refer to the murder of a negative image under sublated male endo-idealism.

Share: Division of goods or services to benefit all participants. Sharing is considered fair if all participants have an equal amount or as much as they want or need. Sharing is typically practised among members of a physical community such as a tribe or family or an endogroup such as a corporation or state. It is distinct from giving, which is the allocation of goods or services the recipient is not socially entitled to.

Shunning: The refusal to recognize, acknowledge or interact with another. Punitive deanimation through the loss of anima conduits.

Singularity: The common definition is of a technological singularity, a time when artificial intelligence will have progressed to the point of a greater-than-human intelligence. The *Binding Chaos* series refers to social or societal singularities to describe society that is already far too complex and requires too much information processing for individual comprehension to be attainable. We now require mass collaboration to understand any aspect of society or to be able to rationally govern ourselves.

Siren: A powerful person who refuses to reflect an idealized image of others and refuses to dispense anima on demand. A negative image.

Society: A tightly bound network of heavily interdependent relationships between people, often used to describe authoritative endogroups.

Solidarity: The (usually revolutionary) demand that reflectors (the Commoners) unquestioningly uphold endoreality.

Sorrow: Sorrow is a result of deanimation. There are three primary types of sorrow: loss sorrow, when euphoric sources are no longer available, expansion sorrow, when exosocial expansion is forced, restricted or diverted, and shame sorrow, when exosocial freedom is lost due to the destruction of self by shame.

Spacetime: The membrane formed around each interaction and the position of interactions relative to each other.

Spirit: An animus, or energy cluster, which may be attached to a self and may be attached to an emotional will but is decoupled from body and usually conscious.

State: Highly militarized partitioning of societies into economic markets imposed for segregating, competing, allocating and establishing property ownership. An endogroup established at the nation self level.

Stigmergy: Action based method of collaboration which follows an idea. If people understand and agree on a goal, everyone has autonomy as to how or whether they work to further that goal. Communication is through transparency. Secrecy and ownership of ideas are in opposition to stigmergy.

Strata slipping: To fall from obedient reflector to negative image status or from endo-ideal to reflector (due to sublation to a transcendental endogroup) or from endo-ideal to negative image (due to revolution).

Strata slumming: Associating or identifying with those one perceives as the negative image. The motivation for strata slumming may be the acquisition of power by migratory endo-ideals, in which case the subject will seek to create an endogroup through demanding recognition from other endo-ideals, or it may be a humiliation fetish, in which case they will seek to further caricature and degrade the group they claim to be a member of.

Stratification: The creation of different classes of society and formation of hierarchy based on roles.

Sublated: The state in which one's interactions and perception of reality are dominated by an external will.

Sublation: The process by which an individual self or an endogroup is merged into a larger endogroup and identifies more strongly with the larger group's endo-ideal than with their earlier self. One side of an interaction is absorbed into the animus of the other and the dominant will receives the majority of anima. Sublation may be to an endo-ideal or endogroup.

Sublator: Predator who dominates the will of another and creates a shared animus through which they freely access the energy of another.

Supranational: Existing above the power of states or nations.

Sympathy: Pity for another as a result of cognitive analysis and moral judgment.

Synthetic euphoria: Euphoria produced by autopredation on a person's own body, through use of drugs or similar.

Systems: Interacting people, ideas, infrastructure and labour which work in a common area, similar to ministries in today's governance. Health, transportation and housing are examples of three different systems. Systems can overlap and cooperate with each other and they have local and global levels. The global level usually acts as an epistemic community of ideas and the local level controls acceptance and rejection of ideas and implementation of them.

Systems of dissociation: Systems constructed to isolate and divide people from their basic needs or each other and their ability to collaborate.

Tall poppy syndrome: The fear, impulse or act of attacking a person who visibly excels above their peers.

Tantalus asceticism: asceticism which causes a slight lessening of the cravings of an endoself by removing from view objects they are unable to possess.

The Taxpayer: The obedient reflector of industrial endo-idealism, closely related to The Working Class and The Honest Hardworking Man. Someone willing to exploit their communities and the unpaid labour of lifegivers and caregivers and employ reversed accounting to accuse others of parasiting off of them. Serves an abstracted endo-ideal anthropomorphized as The Economy.

Third age of nations: A supranational empire where trade has fully abstracted the relationship between oligarchs and the people they exploit.

Thought bubble: A group which is closed to outside thought by forum or propaganda. An endogroup with a strong endoreality.

Time: The attraction or movement between two interactions. This may be synonymous with will.

Torture: An attempt to fully sublate another by instigating a struggle for control over the most intimate circle of self, that containing the body, thoughts, self and life. asceticism under the direction of an external will is torture.

Trade: An endosocial transaction which does not involve connection and is not subject to guilt in the case of imbalance. Trade is conducted between those without the social ties or desire for social ties that accompany sharing or gifting.

Trade economy: An economy which values only goods and services traded to the wealthy and acts as an abstracted force for coercing unbalanced transactions. This creates a form of approval dissociated from society and placed in the hands of the powerful. A method of resource allocation across endosocial barriers.

Trade empire: One which includes an extranational merchant class and is wealthy in large part due to trade.

Trade relationship: An endosocial relationship allowing interactions of unequal force and the accumulation of power.

Transaction: Interactions which do not establish empathic or euphoric conduits through connection but instead facilitate an energy exchange and result in power for the stronger agent.

Transcendence: The sublation of smaller endogroups into a higher authoritative endogroup.

Transcendental endogroup: An endogroup formed through the sublation of smaller endogroups.

Traumatic bond: A bond formed when one will is sublated to another, they share the same animus, or emotional reactions, and are dominated by the same will.

Tribe: A first age nation barely removed from a family structure where all relationships are direct and there is little to no hierarchy or stratification.

Trust networks: A network of people who rely on each other's knowledge and judgment to filter information and sources.

Truth dictatorships: Powerful information sources or endogroups which present one view of reality as a complete 'truth' or 'fact'.

Tyrant: The idol of a power structure in which anima is taken from the masses and given to the idol. An endo-ideal.

User group: The entire population which will be affected by an action, including no one not affected. User groups range from one person to the entire world.

Universal reality:

1. Reality which is outside the subjective viewpoint of the endo-ideal and is not based on the laws of endoreality.

2. Reality which is outside of macroscopic experience.

Vapour capital: Equity, options, intellectual property and rights, or social capital as a product of class such as position, education, citizenship and connections.

Vapour wealth: Conceptual financial wealth, not tied to any physical property.

Violation: An attack on one animus by the will of the other to forcibly extract anima.

Violator: Predator who destroys the personal membrane or connections of another animus so they can access the released energy as secondary anima.

Violence: Forceful violation of bodily autonomy. Violence can be used for the same social purposes as laughter: experience of euphoria, self affirmation, self destruction, social affirmation, social exclusion, endogroup domination and endogroup submission. It also has the same powers as sex: the exosocial power creates strong euphoric and empathic bonds with another person, the endosocial power creates an endosocial membrane, with the subjects joined within the membrane or divided by it, and the endogroup power can be used to sublate one self to another within an endogroup membrane.

Vitality: The health of the life energy of an animus, such as that of a person. Good vitality is the ability to establish and maintain a large and diverse quantity of connections to primary anima. Poor vitality is the blockage of anima conduits and the inability to continue exosocial expansion.

Vitology: The study of life energy.

Volition: The process whereby the conscious will initiates action or intercepts an action initiated by the emotional will to allow or deny its execution.

Wealth: An accumulation of social approval, abstracted or otherwise.

Will: That which chooses. The quantum will controls quantum interactions and it may be sublated to the emotional self (which includes external wills) or the conscious.

Witches: Sources of knowledge or innovation where authoritative power does not want knowledge and innovation.

Wretches: Those hidden from endogroup perspective by the one-way mirror of reflectors and made to absorb all of society's guilt and punishment. The negative image.

Heather Marsh

Index

Index

H

I

T

U

V

W

X

Y

Z

1.

Citations

1. *Burma: End 'Ethnic Cleansing'* of Rohingya Muslims", Human Rights Watch, 22 Apr. 2013.

2. Michels, Robert, *"Political Parties: A Sociological Study of the Oligarchical Tendencies of Modern Democracy"*, Leipzig, 1911

3. Marsh, Heather, *"Obama overrules Amnesty International & President of Yemen, Journalist remains imprisoned"*, WL Central, 12 Feb, 2012

4. Storr, Will, *"The Rape of Men"*, The Guardian, 17 July 2011

5. Massie, Alex, *"In Praise of Sweatshops"*, The Spectator, 26 Apr 2013

6. Mill, John Stuart and Taylor, Harriet, *"On Liberty"*, 1859

7. *"Declaration of the Rights of Man and of the Citizen"*, National Constituent Assembly of France, 26 Aug 1789.

8. *Universal Declaration of Human Rights*, United Nations, 10 Dec 1948

9. *International Covenant on Civil and Political Rights*, United Nations, 16 Dec 1966

10. *International Covenant on Economic, Social and Cultural Rights*, United Nations, 16 Dec 1966

11. Turina, Romana, *"When the system favours the rapist"*, Al Yunaniya, 1 Nov, 2012

12. *"Interview with Pussy Riot Leader: 'I Love Russia, But I Hate Putin"*, Der Speigel , 3 Sept, 2012

13. Elder, Miriam, "*Pussy Riot is the tip of the iceberg – 'there's a lot of intimidation going on'*", The Guardian, 23 Aug 2012

14. Marsh, Heather, *Street maintenance and a cup of tea with police in China*, WL Central, 24 Feb 2011

15. *Boston Marathon Terror Attack Fast Facts*. CNN. Cable News Network. June 3, 2013

16. "*Bangladesh factory collapse toll passes 1,000*", BBC, 10 May 2013

17. Nossiter, Adam, "*Massacre in Nigeria Spurs Outcry Over Military Tactics*", New York Times, 29 Apr 29, 2013

18. Marsh, Heather, *The Rohingya Movement as Seen by a Journalist in Burma*, VICE, Mar 2013

19. Boone, Jeb. "*OpGabon: Anonymous attacks Gabon government sites in protest of ritual killings*", Global Post, 16 Apr, 2013

20. Hollingworth, L. S., *Children above 180 IQ (Stanford-Binet): Origin and development, Yonkers-on-Hudson*, NY: World Book Company, 1942

21. Olson, Parmy, *We Are Anonymous: Inside the Hacker World of LulzSec, Anonymous, and the Global Cyber Insurgency*, Little, Brown and Company, 5 Jun 2012

22. Futrelle, David "*A little gender experiment confirms that Reddit is full of douchebags*" Man Boobz 22 Apr, 2012

23. Smith, S.E., "*Reddit, Free Speech, the Internet and Misogyny*", xo Jane, 15 Oct, 2012

24. Cohen, Noam, "*Define Gender Gap? Look Up Wikipedia's Contributor List*", The New York Times, 30 Jan, 2011

25. "*Uganda Speaks responds to Kony 2012*", Al Jazeera, 21 Apr 2012

26. Bakija, Jon, Cole, Adam, Heim, Bradley T. "Jobs and Income Growth of Top Earners and the Causes of Changing Income Inequality: Evidence from U.S. Tax Return Data", Oct 2010

27. Aristotle, "*Topics*" 350 B.C.E

28. Smith, Adam. *"An Inquiry into the Nature and Causes of the Wealth of Nations"*, 1776

29. Marx, Karl *"Wage Labour and Capital"*, 1847

30. Wollstonecraft, Mary, *"A Vindication of the Rights of Woman"*, 1792

31. Ellison, Marc. "Former Child Soldiers in Uganda Have Renewed Hope for Future." The Star, 9 Sept. 2012

32. Lukhele, Sandile, *"Miniskirts, Tanktops Banned in Swaziland"* Iol News, 24 Dec. 2012

33. Aceh, Banda, *"Indonesian City to Ban Women from Straddling on Motorbikes"* AFP, 2 Jan. 2013

34. Singh, Mahim Pratap, *"Udaipur Muslim Panchayat Bans Mobiles for Girls."* The Hindu, 11 Jan 2013

35. *"School to Prison Pipeline"*, New York Civil Liberties Union, 16 Oct, 2007

36. Kavanagh, Jim, *"Mom jailed for enrolling kids in wrong school district"*, CNN, Jan 26, 2011

37. Laventure, Lisa, *Chinese miners asked to pay for Canadian jobs*, CBC News, 10 Dec, 2012

38. *Pretrial Detention and Torture: Why Pretrial Detainees Face the Greatest Risk*, Open Society Foundations, 2011

39. Pelaez, Vicky, "The prison industry in the United States: big business or a new form of slavery?", Global Research. 2008.

40. Klarreich, Kathie and Polman, Linda. *"The NGO Republic of Haiti"*, The Nation, 31 Oct, 2012

41. *"Will foreign investment aid or exploit Haiti?"* Inside Story Americas, Al Jazeera, 26 Oct 2012

42. *"Freedom From War: The United States Program for General and Complete Disarmament in a Peaceful World"*, U.S.Department Of State, Department Of State Publication 7277, Disarmament Series 5, Sep 1961

43. *"Iraq seen as major arms buyer by 2020"*, UPI.com, 4 Jan, 2013

44. "Basrah Business Delegation Study Tour," Iraq Investment and Reconstruction Task Force (Task Force) of the U.S. Department of Commerce, May 20-24, 2013

45. "Trafficking in Persons Report 2012", US Dept of State, 2012

46. Symons Sarah, *About Slavery*", Made By Survivors, 2013

47. Van Impe, Kristof, *People for Sale: The Need for a Multidisciplinary Approach towards Human Trafficking*", 2013

48. "*International Human Trafficking & Pedophilia*", The Rebecca Project on Human Rights, 2013

49. Ahmad Ayesha, "Mind Trafficking: Child Soldiers in Africa", 02 July, 2008

50. "*Turkish Officials are using Syrians for Organ Harvesting*", Global Research, 05
May, 2013

51. "*Since 2008 there have been 181 ritual killings in Gabon*", Annoying Gabon, 16 April, 2012

52. Locke, John, Second Treatise on Civil Government, 1690

53. Marx, Karl, Engels, Friedrich, "*The Communist Manifesto*", Feb 1848

54. *Institutes of Justinian*, 529 A.D.

55. *Charter of the Forest*, 1217

56. "*La mensajera*", *lavaca*. 10, Dec 2015

57. "*Thoughts on revolution from Take the Square, WL Central and a member of US Day of Rage*", Wikileaks.Central 25, Nov 2011

58. "*Assange can still Occupy centre stage*", Sydney Morning Hareld. 29,Dec 2011

59. "*International media coverage of The Global Square*", Roar Mag. 18, Feb 2012

60. "Radical Realities", Alternate Collective. 22, June 2013

61. Knowles, Jamillah *"Outsiders"*, BBC Radio. 22, Feb 2012

62. *"Audrie & Daisy"*, *Sundance.org.* January 25, 2016

63. Slater, Michael. *"Crime, Justice and Social Media"*, Taylor and Francis. 4 Oct, 2016

64. Miller, Rob. *"The Most Hated Man on the Internet"* 27, July 2022.

The *Binding Chaos* series invites you on a transformative 13-book odyssey. This monumental work is organized into an introductory book and three quartets. Each quartet offers a unique vantage through which to explore different facets of our humanity, searching for the roots of the world we live in. The breadth of research and clarity of focus in this extraordinary work provides an illuminating new viewpoint on the world.

In *The Ontology Quartet*, we explore the five fundamental components that shape who we are and how we interact with society. From historical perspectives to the latest research, a wide and diverse world of knowledge produces innovative and bold new ideas. *The Creation of Me, Them and Us* explores the nature and creation of self, challenging our perceptions and understanding of who we truly are and why we are the way we are. *Abstracting Divinity* takes readers on a remarkable journey through theology, physics, and human nature to show us what we know about life and how that knowledge can be used to guide our choices. *Shaping Reality* ventures into the realm of consciousness and neuroscience to discover the nature of reality. *Free Will and Seductive Coercion* examines our choices, our coercion and the ways in which our paths are chosen.

The Sociology Quartet, brings us from the kernel of our self to the widest expanse of society, breaking down the nature of relationships, power and connection. *The Theft of Self* describes how our interactions create us, and how we are restricted and redirected by our social surroundings. *Great Men, Commoners, Witches and Wretches* explores the roles each person plays in a structure of power. *The Fourth Age of Nations* is a historical look at the evolution of societies with analysis and projection for the future. *Autonomy Diversity Society* offers insights into governance structures.

The Institutions Quartet, investigates the origins and structure of institutions shaping our lives as well as their true effects and purpose. *The Power Economy* dissects economic systems, with a very unique perspective on their nature. *Law and Chaos* looks at the less obvious origins, implications, and purpose of legal systems. *Political Science* investigates the systems, organizations and culture creating authoritative knowledge. *Code Will Rule* explores the ever-expanding role of technology and the world about to be created.

www.ingramcontent.com/pod-product-compliance
Lightning Source LLC
Chambersburg PA
CBHW070903120626
46546CB00001B/122